This series offers the concerned reader basic guidelines and *practical* applications of religion for today's world. Although decidedly Christian in focus and emphasis, the series embraces all denominations and modes of Bible-based belief relevant to our lives today. All volumes in the Steeple series are originals, freshly written to provide a fresh perspective on current—and yet timeless—human dilemmas. This is a series for our times. Among the books:

How to Read the Bible
James Fischer

Soulwinning: An Action Handbook for Christians
Reg A. Forder

A Spiritual Handbook for Women
Dandi Daley Knorr

Temptation: How Christians Can Deal with It
Frances Carroll

*With God on Your Side: A Guide to Finding
Self-Worth Through Total Faith*
Doug Manning

A Daily Key for Today's Christians: 365 Key Texts of the New Testament
William E. Bowles

*Eight Stages of Christian Growth:
Human Development in Psycho-Spiritual Terms*
Philip A. Captain/foreword by Jerry Falwell

How to Pray: Discovering New Spiritual Growth Through Prayer
Barbara A. Gawle

Frustration: How Christians Can Deal with It
Frances Carroll

*How to Talk with God Every Day of the Year:
A Book of Devotions for Twelve Positive Months*
Frances Hunter

*God's Conditions for Prosperity:
How to Earn the Rewards of Christian Living*
Charles Hunter

*A Child of God: Activities for Teaching Spiritual Values
to Children of All Ages*
Peggy D. Jenkins

Prentice-Hall International, Inc., *London*
Prentice-Hall of Australia Pty. Limited, *Sydney*
Prentice-Hall Canada Inc., *Toronto*
Prentice-Hall Hispanoamericana, S.A., *Mexico*
Prentice-Hall of India Private Limited, *New Delhi*
Prentice-Hall of Japan, Inc., *Tokyo*
Prentice-Hall of Southeast Asia Pte. Ltd., *Singapore*
Whitehall Books Limited, *Wellington, New Zealand*
Editora Prentice-Hall do Brasil Ltda., *Rio de Janeiro*

Madeline M. Daniels

Living Your Religion in the Real World

Prentice-Hall, Inc.
Englewood Cliffs, New Jersey 07632

Library of Congress Cataloging in Publication Data

Daniels, Madeline Marie.
   Living your religion in the real world.

   (Steeple books)
   "A Spectrum Book"
   Bibliography: p.
   Includes index.
   1. Christian life—1960–   I. Title.
II. Series.
   BV4501.2.D34 1985   248.4   84-18209
   ISBN 0-13-539016-8
   ISBN 0-13-539008-7 (pbk.)

This book is available at a special discount when ordered
in bulk quantities. Contact Prentice-Hall, Inc., General
Publishing Division, Special Sales, Englewood Cliffs, N.J. 07632.

A SPECTRUM BOOK

Editorial/production supervision by Lori L. Baronian
Cover design ©1985 by Jeannette Jacobs
Manufacturing buyer: Frank Grieco

10 9 8 7 6 5 4 3 2 1

Printed in the United States of America

0-13-539016-8

0-13-539008-7 {PBK}

*To Peter Walden Daniels,
the best friend I've ever had*

Contents

Preface

This book is an integrated approach to living on all dimensions from the spiritual to the physical. Without being mystical, it explores ways to cope with the paradox of being *Homo sapiens*, "the earthly wise ones," and discusses how we can best use our spiritual capacities.

Do you ever feel overwhelmed by the conflicting demands of modern life? Would you like to feel that your life has more direction? Are you tired of being bored or depressed over the meaninglessness of everyday routine? Take heart! This book may help you find the missing connections that can put joy and relevance back into your life.

Designed for readers of all denominations (even agnostics and atheists), this book recognizes that religion is a very personal matter. You're the only one who can choose what is right for you. But this book helps you to make those choices by asking questions that make you think and presenting alternatives to traditional ways of thinking about religion.

This book isn't fancy and it isn't preachy. It is practical and realistic. It talks about some very important dilemmas in plain language. It takes a hard look at your behavior at work and at play, even in the bedroom. With your collaboration, it can help you integrate all the aspects of your life into a meaningful whole.

There are exercises and suggestions to help you apply your religious beliefs to everyday situations at work, at home, at play. This book explores the challenges of living, but it also explores the joy in living. It encourages the reader to develop all the potential inherent in being human, but it recognizes play as being as much a part of this task as work.

Few books on religion attempt to deal with such a diversity of topics in such matter-of-fact language. But only by facing up to all our varied complexities can we achieve the sense of harmony we feel when we truly understand our place in the universe. By viewing life as a divine dance, we can find enjoyment, as well as significance, in our attempts to balance our earthly and spiritual sides.

This book isn't the last word on religion, nor does it claim to be a divinely revealed word. Instead, it approaches religion as a reflection of our human need to recognize the cosmic connections that link us all to each other and the universe beyond. Thought provoking, frequently controversial, it asks you, the reader, to participate in reevaluating and recreating your partnership with the cosmic.

Madeline M. Daniels, author of *Realistic Leadership* (Prentice-Hall, 1983), is the executive director of the Crossroads Center, a counseling and consulting firm in East Kingston, New Hampshire. In addition to conducting workshops and in-service training, she frequently lectures at the University of New Hampshire.

1

The Earthly Wise Ones

This is a book for members of the species *Homo sapiens.*
The word *homo*, which distinguishes our primate genus,
is taken from an old Latin word meaning "the earthly
one" and is related to the Latin word *humus*, which
means "earth" or "soil"; the second word, *sapien*, means
"wise." Presumably, then, we are the wise ones of this
earth. Yet all of us have felt overwhelmed at times by the
complexities of modern life. We know how foolish we
can feel when confronted by conflicting demands. We are
a thinking species, yet nonlogical impulses often have
more of an influence on our behavior than rational
thought. We often think in terms of opposites—good/
bad, work/play, body/spirit—and then can't seem to reconcile the way we act with the way we think.

We often cope with the demands of our life by splitting them up into little boxes and behaving differently in
each one. As we pass through the office box, the home
box, the church box, the disco box, we force ourselves to
change behaviors to suit the demands imposed by each
individual box. This kind of inconsistency takes a toll on

us. It saps our energy, disrupts our health, confuses our relationships with people, and erodes our image of ourselves.

Our century has been faced with a variety of epidemics that all appear related to this inconsistent pattern of responses. We complain of future shock, stress-related illnesses, identity crises, depression, apathy, and anxiety. Sometimes life's simple pleasures don't seem to exist anymore. There is pressure to watch what we eat, how much we drink, how we have sex; too many demands, too many possibilities. How did we get into this mess anyway? And how do we get out?

Human Beings Are Too Adaptable for Their Own Good

As a species, we are characterized by our highly developed brain and its capabilities. We can do more than any other species. We can adjust to any climate, any geography, any social structure. We have created a multitude of cultures and enough paraphernalia to clutter the earth indefinitely. (This paraphernalia is often called "material culture" or "tools.") We have proved our ability to withstand any disaster and overcome any obstacle. But as modern individuals, we often feel we have lost something. Why?

Simply because we are so adaptable! As a group, humans have run around reacting rather than planning ahead. As individuals, we tend to function the same way. You've heard of "management by exception"? (This is the style of managing by reacting only to emergencies rather than planning ahead to prevent them.) Well, have you ever felt you're living by exception? Adapting to each new demand or requirement, rather than planning ahead to create the most enjoyable life possible?

We wouldn't begin a building without a blueprint, but we often build our lives without planning or forethought of any kind. We get so good at adapting to each new obstacle that we never stop to ask, "Why? Where am I going?" Then one day, if we are honest people, the inconsistencies of our lives catch up with us, and we are panicked by their apparent meaninglessness.

This book is designed to go back to basic questions. It tries to help you plot a direction for your life. It asks questions that may cut through accumulated inconsistencies to your basic values and needs. It can help you see through trivia and recognize meaning. There is no one answer to the question of how you live religion in the everyday world, because we all carry a different answer in our soul. This book is an exploration of that soul and its impact on your daily activities.

We busy ourselves with adapting to our environment from the time we are born. We explore our home and family and learn their limitations. At first we are creative in our approach; we touch and taste everything in sight. But the external world imposes boundaries on our explorations: "Don't do that! Don't touch that! Be careful or you'll get hurt!" If we refrain from exploration, most often it is because we fear our family's disapproval. (Rarely are we permitted to actually hurt ourselves.) Many of the limits are indeed necessary ones. The point is that we learn to adapt to them long before we understand their necessity.

In later years, we fear the disapproval of peers and authority figures in the business world or our community. We substitute one for the other from force of habit. The result is that we are often still acting like children, fearing without knowing why.

We learn some unnecessary rules along with the needed ones. At an age when we cannot analyze or evaluate, we simply adapt to fit in with what we are told. When we grow older, we may continue to adapt without thinking. We are told we need to earn a living, so we focus on adapting to the workplace. We leave at five and are told we should spend time with our family, so we shift gears and focus on that. We are told we should plan for the future, we are told we should enjoy the present, but rarely does anyone tell us how we can do all these things at once without collapsing from exhaustion.

If we adapt to each specific situation as it arises, and all situations that arise, we may become like squirrels frantically gathering nuts for winter, only to forget where they are buried because they tried to do too much at once. To paraphrase an old saying about work, maybe the answer is to live smarter, not harder.

Adaptation versus Integration

Let's look at an example. Most people in our society are raised with some kind of formal religious training. This training may encourage or discourage an integrated view of the world. We are taught in church or synagogue about a set of rules and models that are supposed to be important. They may be taught as ancient history, with no relation (that a child can see) to modern life. We may learn rituals that we see our parents do not understand. We may be given rules—"Love they neighbor" or "Thou shalt not bear false witness," for example. Then we see adults violating those rules without thought.

Unless our religious training has been well integrated into our family's life, we may learn early to adapt by giving lip service to the rules without thinking about the meaning. Then we grow up and enter the business world. We adapt very well. We play office politics and talk about putting one over on the boss. We lie to the Internal Revenue Service, and we lie to our boss about why we were out yesterday.

But we still go back to the church or synagogue (or send our children or our money in our place). We believe in the religious teachings with one part of ourselves, and in the business teachings with another. We separate ourselves into pieces and then wonder why we feel fragmented and uncomfortable. We treat our lovers differently from our spouses, our children differently from our grandchildren, and we go on splitting our world and ourselves into tinier pieces until there is nothing left that we can call our true self.

This is a compromise between what we learn with our minds and what we learn from the "real world." We persuade ourselves that "that stuff is okay, but it doesn't work in the real world." We put all our energy into the constant compromises required by the different boxes we have built. What if we put that same energy into integrating the various things we have learned into a meaningful whole instead?

As the species' name indicates, we are both earthly (*i.e.*, physical world) and wise (*i.e.*, nonphysical). We know there is more to life than survival. This book is for those who wish to *live*, rather than merely exist. It deals with religion as a real issue, because without religion we are no better than joyless machines. It approaches the integration of religion and the everyday world with a focus on practicality. It is designed to help you, the reader, design your own blueprint for building a life of meaning and wholeness.

Religion has been the term we have used to cover a broad spectrum of ideas and variables. It has come to have many meanings, and for many of us, it represents the blueprint from which we should build our lives. But many feel that religion does not function as a blueprint because the measurements and designs are outdated and impractical in a modern setting. In other words, many people do not take the time to examine and convert the diagrams into modern day applications.

What Is Religion?

In this book, we will learn to understand the various components that make the concept of *religion*. It is a difficult word to define to everyone's satisfaction. One way of understanding religion is to look at the word itself. *Religion* is related to the Latin word for "to tie, to fasten together." It is used to refer to beliefs and world views that we use to tie the world together. Religion means connection. It makes sense of the world and our place in it.

As humans, we go beyond mere adaptation when we try to understand our connection to the universe. Science seeks to understand, so that it can predict. Religion seeks to understand the unpredictable. I'd like to distinguish between the two kinds of understanding. We might call the first kind "knowledge," and the second kind "wisdom." Knowledge, of the scientific kind, is vital if our species is to grow to its fullest potential. But wisdom, of the religious kind, is vital if the individual is to grow to her or his fullest potential.

Most of us realize the value of knowledge. But not everyone has stopped to realize that knowledge is not wisdom. We may have the knowledge to create a new technology, but not the wisdom to use it well. The individual may have the knowledge needed to survive, but not the wisdom to live in joy and harmony. Without a feeling of connectedness, all the knowledge we can accumulate may seem empty and meaningless.

Oscar Wilde once said, "A cynic is one who knows the price of everything and the value of nothing." In other words, a cynic has knowledge but not wisdom. In Chapter Eight, we'll take a look at the impact of knowledge used unwisely and of wisdom ignored. Without a healthy set of values, our technological knowledge may bring destruction rather than creation.

Many people reach that sense of connectedness without having a formal religious affiliation, or even believing in a god/being. Even within the crowd of organized religions, we find as wide a diversity of images as we find human cultures in the world. We find god or goddess, one or many, and pictures of each as varied as individuals in a crowd. In order to better discuss religion as a whole, we need to look at its various possible components.

Let us use the following model: Religion is composed of three distinct spheres—ethics, spirituality, and congregation. Any given person or group may put these components together to help reach a feeling of connection within their world.

Ethics refers largely to our connection to things we see outside ourselves: how we treat objects, people (even strangers), animals, our environment, and so on. It is used to refer to our values and priorities and how we translate those values into behavior toward the outside, visible world. Questions of right and wrong, good and bad, how we "should" act—these are ethical concerns.

Spirituality refers to our sense of connection with all that exists, even that which cannot be seen with our physical senses. It suggests a specialness, an awe-filled sense of having a more-than-physical connection with the cosmos. Anthropologists often use the term *numinous* to refer to this sense of a spark of divinity. It does not have to refer to belief in a particular spirit or spirits, but rather to the belief that something exists above and beyond the physical. (One way of saying this is, "The whole is greater than the sum of its parts." For example, any good neurologist can tell you that the mind appears to be more than the sum of the physical brain.)

Congregation refers to the desire and need of people to create a more personal connection with other people. They may do this by identifying themselves as a group, sharing common beliefs or a common tradition. It is the social aspect of religion, group behavior rather than individual perceptions that can create a sense of almost family-like connectedness, an extension of individual, one-to-one friendships.

Your own particular religion may focus on any one of these three aspects, or any combination of them. Many people, for example, focus primarily on rational ethical behavior. Within this focus, they may function as individuals without a group, or create a group for the purpose of supporting social change. (Some Unitarians illustrate this type of focus.) Others may focus largely on the congregational aspects of religion, allowing group leaders to set ethical behavior or define appropriate spirituality. (Some Catholics might illustrate this pattern.)

Even within religions that have a tendency toward a particular pattern, local congregations may display a different emphasis. The important things to consider are these:

1. These three areas provide a useful way of understanding religion by comparing their ingredients.
2. All of the above characteristics are distinctly human, and two of them—ethics and spirituality—appear to be uniquely human.
3. The primary purpose of religion is for us to feel a sense of connection; these components are the tools we use to help us in this goal.

This book is intended to explore some general guidelines for applying religion to your life. Because of the diversity of religions, readers must take the time to examine their own religious values and feelings and use these guidelines to build an integrated life. In this book, we will discuss basic examples from each category, examples that are common enough to be recognized by many readers. But there are several reasons why we will keep to discussing guidelines rather than specifics.

One reason is that using examples important to only one religious group would not be useful to readers who are members of other groups. We all use different metaphors and myths to illustrate our world views. Like the pieces of a jigsaw puzzle, they must all be considered simultaneously if we are to comprehend the range of human vision of the divine.

A second reason is that this book is being written from a comparative point of view, not a judgmental one.

"By their fruits shall ye know them" (Mt. 12:33) is the viewpoint in this book. No individual or group is evaluated by *what* is believed, but rather by *how* the beliefs affect the connection that religion is meant to encourage.

A third reason for discussing guidelines, rather than choosing one specific religion, is this: a healthy balance among the three components is often discussed in theory but seems to be harder to achieve in practice. While it may be difficult to locate an organized religious tradition with whom we agree 100 percent, we can find individuals of many faiths who appear to be happy and healthy with what we might call a good set of connections! (The pun is intentional.)

No single religious affiliation seems to have all the answers. But within every organized group are some individuals who have worked out guidelines for living every day to the fullest. Let's try to benefit from all their different experiences.

Do You Have to Be a Mystic to Find Harmony and Balance?

Each of us treads a different path through different woods. There is no one map that would be helpful to everyone. But if you know how to read a compass and draw a map, you can create your own drawing of your own place. It may be slightly different from someone else's, but the important thing is that it leads you through the woods, without the terror of feeling lost with night approaching.

This is a book for those who wish to have the skills to create their own maps. Years of studying religions and people have convinced me that you don't have to run off to a cloister or a Tibetan ashram to live your religion. It might seem nice to get away from the distractions that seem to make it difficult to find meaning in everyday life. But then again, it may be more fulfilling to live in both (or all) worlds at once. We may grow more if we have to keep exploring the world daily, finding creative ways to integrate our religious feelings with more mundane realities. Each can give vitality to the other.

One of the basic perspectives of this book is that harmony means balancing all the various possible options. Being well balanced does not mean that you must lead a dull, middle-of-the-road existence, avoiding extremes entirely. Harmony in music allows for different notes, different tempos, and both loud and soft sections within the whole composition. So, too, should life have variety. But a well-composed musical composition does not jerk from one extreme to another; whether the notes blend or contrast, the movement flows together.

In dance, the word for this kind of harmony is *grace*; we speak of a dancer being graceful when he or she can execute a variety of movements so they flow together. It is interesting to note that we use this same word, *grace*, as a particularly religious term. The word comes from Latin roots that connote "favor" and "esteem," as well as "pleasing." One could almost suggest that we see someone in harmony as participating in a divine favor. The state of grace and gracefulness seem to have harmony and balance as an underlying theme.

The Hindu religion has a particularly vivid metaphor for illustrating this state. The god Shiva is said to be dancing each of us. In other words, each of us is a dance: an active process, not just a static being. We are the active motion of God. But he does it so well that (like a good actor) he sometimes forgets that he is Shiva, and begins to think he *is* the person he is dancing. When we forget that we are really a performance of the divine, we lose our connection with the cosmic dance. A Christian might say that Christ lives in every one of us. When we forget that, we lose our sense of the reality of our own divine essence.

What each of these metaphors is saying is that we feel and act least graceful when we feel unconnected to a larger whole. It is not that we do not exist as individuals; we are not a figment of a divine imagination. We exist rather as *both* unique individuals *and* as a part of a cosmic pattern. We cannot develop our fullest potential if we do not remember the first fact, but we cannot be truly at peace if we forget the second.

One of my favorite quotations that expresses this idea of connectedness is by John Donne. In modern language, it reads:

> No one is an island, entire of itself. Each human is a piece of the continent, a part of the whole. If a clod be washed away by the sea, the continent is the lesser, as much as if a promontory were. Any one's death diminishes me, because I am involved in Humankind. And therefore never send to know for whom the bell tolls, it tolls for thee.

This sense of involvement, of being connected to all other people, can even be extended into feeling a sense of connectedness with all things. We have learned, too harshly, the dangers of not seeing our interdependence with our environment. Perhaps the religious, cosmic sense of being related is an important antidote to the disease that modern life so often evokes. Illness is often caused by this lack of feeling comfortable with our world.

Describing illness as dis-ease emphasizes the need to be spiritually healthy in order to be physically healthy.

Soul-Sickness

Why can't we cope better with our own world? Those who have become adults in this century have dealt with world wars, Great Depression, bombs that can depopulate a continent, and a technology that evolves faster than we can understand it. Our parents remember a different world from the one our children are familiar with. We know there are more things available to us, even if we don't always have the time or the money to try them. Our kids live in two-car families with color televisions, but we're not always sure they're better off than we were.

Often we aren't even sure we're better off. Is today's world really better? It seems that things have changed so fast that we are only just beginning to think about the trade-offs we have had to make. We struggle for years to do the things we must do, then often look around in midlife and wonder why we are doing them. If we are doing things right, shouldn't we feel happier?

Over and over I see people struggling with these questions. I've come to call it "soul-sickness." You won't find it in the medical or psychiatric manuals, but it exists just the same. It is characterized by a feeling of confusion, a loss of self-understanding (identity crisis), a sense of meaninglessness, and the death of hope. It is often accompanied by a lack of religious beliefs, though it is as likely to occur in members of the clergy as it is in atheists.

It can occur in average people who can't seem to reconcile what they were taught in school or church with the way things are (or seem to be): people who mean to do well, but don't understand why their behavior isn't consistent with what they would like to be (or were told to be). We have already discussed how soul-sickness can occur, what its symptoms are, and why religion—the one area designed to cure it—often fails to work. We are talking about a lack of a blueprint to work from, and this book is meant to help us use the knowledge and the information you already have to try to reconstruct that blueprint for yourself. This book will suggest an approach that I choose to call "sapience," the particular type of wisdom associated with being human.

Sapience: A Cure for Soul-Sickness

Why create a new word when there are so many words already scattered around? Because the concept discussed in this book is not adequately described by any existing word. They all have too many other associations. I needed a word to suggest wisdom (as distinct from knowledge) and a particular state of harmony and grace associated with that kind of wisdom. Sapience suggests, as well, a quality of wisdom and harmony that is uniquely human.

The word *humanism* I discarded because it has too often been usurped by total rationalists who completely discount any spiritual aspects of humanity. Still, the concept of developing sapience is a practical and realistic approach. What could be more real than developing *all* the potential of being human—both the physical and the nonphysical?

Another problem was finding a word that was not gender linked. If feminism is the belief that women deserve the human right to develop their full potential and have equal access to all opportunities, where is the word that gives both sexes that right? Sapience denotes the rights of both genders to be fully human, to grow and develop all their individual capabilities.

Since the sapient approach suggests a variety of techniques to achieve its goal, it might be called "wholistic." But that word is associated largely with an emphasis on physical well-being. It has also been associated, in the minds of many, with some of the less scientifically sound methods which use that word. A word was needed that has not been used in connection with an already existing movement, to avoid being confused with inappropriate associations.

What sapience suggests is a blending of knowledge and awareness, a logical approach to the nonlogical. It requires that you stop and think ahead, rather than live by exception. It suggests that in order to make the most of being human, you have to accept all that it means to be human.

This doesn't mean you simply accept all of life's evils and stop trying to change them. You don't agree to allow murder or starvation or pollution. It means that you start the process of change from within, by understanding yourself. If you change your own attitudes and accept your cosmic connectedness, you may find it easier to have an impact on those external events you want to change.

Perhaps if we all focused more on the wisdom inside of ourselves, the world would grow a little faster. I'm not talking about those who claim revealed knowledge and try to force their "knowledge" onto others. I'm talking about a world in which we all recognize that our souls are connected, and that we are all part of the divine. Just as we are unlikely to chop off our own arm or leg, so too might we stop injuring our neighbor and our environment.

We have feelings and we have rationality. We have science and we have religion. We have internal thoughts and dreams and we have external relationships. We are physical and nonphysical. In order to achieve a feeling of connectedness, it is first essential to stop fighting your humanness and accept being one of the "earthly wise ones."

2

The Work Ethic and the Work Mystique

When people think of religion, the last place they think of is the place where they work. Nobody associates religion with the workplace. People put business and religion in separate rooms in their heads. One thing has nothing to do with the other! Rarely do people in their place of business feel like part of a congregation dedicated to a higher goal. Rarely do we get a feeling of mystical joy from our business endeavors. And few would disagree with the observation that the ethical precepts that most of us associate with religion are routinely ignored in our workplaces.

Few people expect anything different from their job. Most people are satisfied if they simply get along with co-workers. Very few people have even considered the possibility of work being a joyous and sacred experience. And as for ethics, ask yourself the following questions: How comfortable do most people feel with their actions and thoughts in the workplace? Have you ever compared how you behave at work with how you behave outside of work? Or, worse yet, with how you think you should behave?

The Seven Deadly Vices and Worker Discontent

What if we looked at office behavior through an ethical analysis? You may have learned about the Seven Deadly Vices as part of early religious training. Chances are that you have filed them away in your head as a useless and archaic list. But suppose we take a new look at people's behavior in the workplace, using these terms: *greed, pride, unkindness, sloth, dishonesty, cowardice,* and *lust.*

If you are a manager on any level, you may find it easy to label your subordinates' behavior in these categories. In the interest of fairness, let's make a special effort to balance this with a clear recognition of the vices that managers fall prey to. Are you ready to look at your place of business through this new perspective? It may be painful, but you may find it more relevant than you realize.

1. Greed is easy to spot in the workplace. We all want a bigger paycheck, a better title, a larger office, another assistant. By calling this greed "ambition," we allow ourselves to have mixed emotions. We applaud someone's competitive spirit, but might worry whether she or he was too ambitious. What if we just labeled the desire to acquire more of anything as *Greed*, pure and simple? Can you be honest enough with yourself to see when you are motivated by greed?

If we focus our attention on the material things we want to get from our job, we distract ourselves from thinking about how well we do the job, what we are learning from the job, or how our co-workers feel about their part in doing the job. By caring only about what we get, we end up ignoring all the other valuable results of working.

this results in competition with others for a "piece of the action," our "slice of the pie." We cease to care about balance or growth or harmony. This attitude hurts ourselves, and hurts the whole company. An emphasis on acquisition can be seen as plain old-fashioned Greed, and considered a vice because of its effect.

Managers must realize that anyone moving "up the ladder of success" is especially prone to this vice. What is even worse is that competition among managers and departments can set a poor example for everyone in the company. You can hardly criticize subordinates for wanting more if you have set an example of greed and acquisitiveness. Many companies have run into serious problems when their original purpose gets lost in a battle to see whether employees or employers get a bigger share of the profits.

This doesn't mean it is wrong to want to earn a livelihood or be safe and comfortable while you work. It's just that if we relabel ambition by a less vague name, people might have to think about why they were fighting for more material possessions. Is it need or greed?

2. Pride is another vice often seen at the workplace. It usually manifests itself in a stubborn refusal to admit mistakes. Even though we all know that "to err is human," many people have an unrealistic fear of being wrong. They blame others when problems occur. They refuse to say, "I don't know." They presume they have the right to judge, criticize, or ridicule others.

Setting yourself up as better than others puts distance between you and them. It discourages people from sharing their honest thoughts and feelings with you. It is also a drain on your energy to constantly pretend to be perfect. Pride creates loneliness and isolation for yourself and fear and resentment in those whom you blame. It prevents growth, learning, and cooperation.

It is unfortunate that most of the terms we use to talk about business tend to encourage this false distance. We talk about the boss, subordinates, white-collar, and blue-collar labor. Words like these suggest inequality. But having different functions in an organization does not automatically make one function better than another. I've heard people refer to themselves as "just a secretary" or "just an assembler." But these are the jobs that keep the company producing!

We all know that a failure in a tiny hose or valve in our car can stop the whole engine from working. The smallest part in the machine may be vital to its performance. Businesses are like that, too. The job of manager exists only because of the people who do the work that needs managing. Being able to organize their work is not a higher skill, only a different one. All skills are important to a smoothly running operation.

3. Unkindness is next on our list. Notice how rarely we consider the feelings of the people with whom we work. Our whole business system is built on treating people as if they were not human while working. If we are motivated by greed and pride, we tend to give no thought to the needs of our co-workers.

We often see more than just thoughtlessness in daily business interaction. Many people speak to their subordinates or co-workers with such harshness that you wonder if they realize the damage they are doing. Creating unnecessary friction wrecks the smooth functioning of the office team. Unkindness can kill an employee's motivation, and destroy the morale of the whole team. Being unkind shows a poor understanding of how to teach people and how to motivate them.

If all workers, with all their varying skills are needed to maintain a project, then unkindness on the part of a manager can have devastating effects. If the role of a manager is to provide organization and support for the team, unkindness is stupid. Rigidity is not organization, and thoughtlessness is not support.

Often what is lacking is just a knowledge of communication skills or competency with people. Yet many managers show their unkindness by refusing to learn these skills. But if both people and tasks need managing, then ignoring people-skills makes you only half a manager.

4. Sloth, the next Deadly Vice, is reaching epidemic proportions today. We hear it called apathy, poor morale, lack of motivation, and lack of craftsmanship in one's work. Sometimes it manifests itself as "keeping a low profile"; in other words, doing the minimum necessary to keep a job, without putting energy into creative improvements. Sometimes it just takes the form of spending more time on breaks than at the desk.

In any case, sloth obviously makes life harder for co-workers. More important, it destroys the self-respect of the person committing it. Work doesn't get done, deadlines aren't met, and other people may have to take up the slack. There can be no self-satisfaction in a job not done, so nobody benefits from an apathetic worker.

It may be easy for a manager to complain about the

laziness of workers, but how many set a good example themselves? Employees do notice how much time the boss spends on lunches or in unproductive meetings. If half that time were spent listening to employee problems and helping them reach constructive solutions, more real work might be accomplished. If extended business lunches or business trips are a necessary part of the job, it might help to educate workers on exactly what these things accomplished.

It is often amazing how many companies suffer from sloth when it comes to keeping workers informed. It often seems like too much trouble to tell people exactly what the company is doing, where their job fits into the overall pattern, or what other people's roles are. Yet lack of this information reduces their interest and encourages apathy. A lazy attitude on the part of management breeds laziness throughout.

5. Dishonesty is another commonly ignored vice at the workplace. Cheating on time sheets or expense accounts is expected. Stealing office supplies for home use is often considered a fair game. Employers easily recognize these forms of dishonesty.

But how often does upper management fail to see their own dishonesty? Expecting salaried employees to work overtime on a regular basis steals their time. Failure to disseminate information about office goals or problems is lying. Refusing to listen to the problems of workers is cheating them by refusing to provide the support they need to do the most effective job. And giving lip service to encourage creative thinking while discouraging any new ideas is the worst dishonesty of all.

Concrete examples come readily to mind. Take the company that instituted profit-sharing as an incentive to workers. Much fuss was made over the idea that workers had a right to be aware of and share in the fruits of their labor. The idea worked, profits increased, and a hefty check was presented to each worker the first year. Next year's checks were even bigger. Employees were delighted with the results of their efforts. So what did the company do next?

The cwners, in effect, decided that they hadn't meant for workers to make that much of a profit! Without consulting the employees, they decided to turn the profit-sharing plan into a penison-type plan. Now, instead of a tangible check once a year, workers could only touch their money at the end of ten or twenty years. People felt they had been lied to. Credibility vanished, morale dropped, and the turnover rate for workers sky-rocketed.

6. Cowardice is such an accepted part of our attitude towards our jobs that we often fail to see it as such. Some workers (and managers!) make a virtue of "not rocking the boat." They fear conflict, so they run away from every potential disagreement. They are afraid to confront other people about their problems, so the problems are never solved.

Cowardice invariably confuses any issue. If you are really bothered by something in your office, not talking about it may lead others to think you accept it. If you try to talk to your boss, and give in at the first sign of resistance, your boss may think the problem solved when it isn't. If you feel resentful, your internal or external griping may make the situation worse.

Cowardice can take the opposite form. Rigidly sticking to your ideas and refusing to even consider the other person's point of view is also a sign of fear. Avoiding a conflict by imposing a solution on employees can show that you are afraid to argue the merits of your ideas. Or that you are afraid of emotions, either yours or theirs. Many people have stifled their input at a problem-solving meeting for fear of being wrong or even of just looking foolish.

Many managers are frightened of human emotions. They avoid the problem by saying things like "Emotions have no place at the office." Since human beings work in offices, and since human beings have emotions, emotions are a fact of life at the office. Pretending they don't exist shows cowardice. People will feel happy or sad, comfortable or uncomfortable, friendly or angry. Cowardice in dealing with those feelings has sabotaged many a business project.

7. Lust is perhaps the most complex of the vices. If we think of it in terms of coveting something that someone else has, perhaps we can see why it causes so much confusion in the workplace. We lust for power, we lust for sex, we want something from another person. In defining a desire as a vice, let us be clear that the real danger lies in the hidden nature of lust.

Saying "I'd like a date with you" or "I'd like to go to bed with you" is not necessarily a vice because it is open and grants freedom of choice to the other person. Even saying "I'd like to have your office" or "I envy you your job" is not a sign of lust/envy. The vice lies in keeping these feelings secret, while doing everything you can to manipulate the situation to get these things.

Lust causes confusion because it hides your true reasons for your actions. It robs the other person of freedom of choice by refusing to present them with a clear choice. In cases where the lust is for sexual relations, it can force an untenable choice, as in, "Have sex with me or lose your job." By confusing others as to your motives, by misleading them into potentially harmful decisions, it is a crime against their dignity and self-respect.

God Isn't Dead; God's Bored

Does all this analysis of business behavior from the standpoint of Seven Deadly Vices seem important to you? Or do you feel that it is harsh to label typical feelings and actions as *Vices*? The moral of this section may be that if we honestly examine life in an everyday workplace, we may become aware of exactly how badly we behave there.

You can't expect to make work a joyous and rewarding experience if you treat it as a separate box where the usual rules don't apply. If work is to be a relevant and meaningful part of your life, then it must be integrated into the whole of your beliefs. Treating your job as a chore which must be endured but which is unrelated to the rest of your life is asking your soul to be bored.

Social scientists often talk about the difference between *sacred* and *profane*. Their definitions of these categories might be useful to help us understand why we bore our soul to death at the office. *Sacred* refers to the quality of spirituality we discussed in Chapter One, that sense of the special and the numinous. An experience can feel sacred when we notice that spark of the divine within ourselves.

It need not be only a pleasant experience. Some things that are negative can stir us to a recognition of the sacred by their intensity. Murder can shock us into recognizing the value of human life. Taboos against incest or desecration of holy places help remind us of our strong respect for the family or our traditions. In other words, something powerfully terrifying can trigger our feelings of the connectedness of the world if we feel strongly upset when that connectedness is violated.

By contrast, the term *profane* refers to the mundane world, the nonexcitement of everyday events. It refers to the banal, the boring, the petty, and the trivial. There is a certain security in having everything be routine and ordinary. If things are of little importance, there are no risks and no surprises. But there is also no excitement. As the saying goes: "Behold the turtle who only makes progress when he sticks his neck out."

Most of us place work and the office routine strictly in the category of the profane. We say it is important because we need the money, or we say it is exciting because it is a high-stress job, but our actual attitudes and actions while working are clearly nonsacred. Our work is not considered of divine importance because we separate it from all the other aspects of our life. We treat our job profanely because we don't allow ourselves to see any significance in everyday actions.

Yet we spend most of our waking hours at the workplace. We chase a petty power within the company's political structure instead of valuing the real power that comes from getting a job done and thus having an impact on the world. We allow ourselves to be apathetic, accepting office policy rather than rocking the boat by being creative. We compete with co-workers for money and position rather than focusing on the cooperation needed to get the job done.

We stifle the free exchange of ideas and feelings; we ignore the chance to learn more about ourselves and others. If we look at our discussion of the Seven Deadly Vices, we realize that ethics have ceased to have any meaning at the office. We fear to disagree or state a strong opinion on anything. In short, we fear to make a commitment to what we are doing. We bore our souls to death.

Must You Feel Bad to Be Good?

Is it possible to look at our jobs in a way that gives them meaning? Can we begin to see the sacredness behind the coat of mundanity we have painted over the workplace? At present, it often seems we are offered just two choices in our attitudes towards work: The Work Ethic and The Work Mystique.

The Work Ethic is the current version of the old Puritan Ideal. "It's good to work hard." "In the sweat of thy brow, thou shalt earn thy daily bread," and so on. Traditionally, work is something you struggle with, either as a punishment for your sins or as a learning experience in self-discipline. The more you hate your job, the more praise you get for sticking with it. Like medicine, the worse it tastes, the better it's supposed to be for you!

But is this really the truth? I'll bet you know lots of people who go out for tennis or other sports. If you throw yourself into a tennis game and sweat, you can feel really good both psychologically and physically. Some people even throw themselves into such exhausting "work" to get away from the office grind. So work and sweat can't be synonymous because you can play and sweat, and you can work without sweating.

The ultimate Puritan response is probably that it is sinful to enjoy your work. We look askance at writers, actors, artists, and musicians who seem to be having a good time when they should be "working." Part of our disapproval is rooted in envy that they may be enjoying themselves while earning their livelihood, instead of being miserable like we are. The other part of our disapproval may be our fear that if we were enjoying ourselves, we wouldn't be "productive." And lack of productivity is the great American sin, thanks largely to our Puritan heritage.

The Work Mystique is our modern alternative to the Work Ethic. The office is considered a place apart from other realities. It may be dreary or just barely tolerable. It may even be considered a fun game, if you play by the rules. But the rules are different from any other sphere of our lives. Getting ahead on the job becomes all important, and all other values just don't exist in the workplace.

This isolation of work from other parts of our lives trivializes forty or more hours a week of our existence. Worse yet, it creates a lack of harmony and balance that we often frantically try to correct. We work for the house or for the vacation or for retirement. By always promising ourselves a future goal, we lose the joy and sacredness that is possible in the present.

Other people go for more immediate rewards. They lose themselves in sports after work, or come alive only on weekends. They collect material goods as proof of the value of their work. But what good is wearing a two-hundred dollar dress to an eight-hour day that has no meaning beyond that dress? What good is the microwave oven that cooks a frozen meal on a paper plate in order to regain time lost by working extra hours to buy the oven?

Both the Work Ethic and the Work Mystique ignore the possibility that work could be both fun and productive, both meaningful and delightful. Like the tennis game, your business activities require effort and planning to achieve these goals. Spontaneous play is a joy and a delight, but even the ability to play when the mood strikes is greatly encouraged by the forethought to have the necessary "toys" ready and waiting.

If you are willing to accept that work can be a positive part of your life, you must be willing to spend at least as much time preparing for it as you do for your sports and hobbies. In Chapter Three, we'll be looking at ways to actually make your work consistent with your ideas and feelings. But it will take effort on your part. There's no magic solution, just the need for clearly defined goals and consistent planning ahead.

If you don't get your tennis racket fixed when the string breaks, you won't be able to play next time you get the chance. Why do we avoid planning ahead for work the same way? Planning ahead to give meaning to our work would have far more impact on our lives than planning for a two-hour tennis match.

What's the Point of Working Anyway?

One of the reasons people fail to give work the same attention they give their play is because they define them as two different things. Like the Hindu god Shiva we mentioned in Chapter One, we tend to forget that we are dancing. We lose the divine spark within us that sees the playful interaction between all things. We stop seeing the beauty and sacredness around us.

Some people have looked at our current attitudes toward work and chosen to try to avoid the whole issue.

Is this really a solution? Few of us would really like to be the hobo without responsibilities but without a home and family. Total avoidance of work is not only difficult to achieve but it tends to leave you cold, hungry, and lonely.

But what about the generation of flower children who valued friendship and ideals without wanting to buy into the Work Ethic or the Work Mystique? Certainly some hippies finally gave up and got a job on Wall Street. Maybe they just became part of the problem they were trying to solve. But what about the people who tried hard to obtain the things they valued?

You may know people who tried to homestead land or became part of a commune or extended family. If so, you know the first thing that happened was the realization that it wasn't as easy as it seemed. That was the time when some people gave up and either dropped out of society entirely or dropped back into the society they had tried to run away from.

But some people kept on trying. They thought about what they wanted out of life, and they were willing to put energy into getting it. Those who worked at putting their ideals into practice kept seeking out alternative ways of providing for their daily needs. Little by little, many of them are building lives that they are happy with, while constantly exploring new ways of accomplishing their goals.

There are historical precedents for this. Monasteries and abbeys consist of people finding meaning in their individual lives while working together to provide for the necessities of daily life. So do Buddhist ashrams and Tibetan lamaseries. In many ways, it seems easier to do this when you are living in a closed community of people who support you in this effort.

Looking at these kinds of lives, it becomes clear that we have another definition of work. Work can simply be anything you put energy into. You can work at playing. (Remember our sweaty tennis player?) Work can be hard, but it can be intrinsically rewarding. If what you are doing to earn a livelihood is consistent with your ideals and values, and contains activities that you like, then your job becomes a meaningful part of your life.

It's simple, isn't it? You work because you are alive. Life is motion and activity as well as rest and peace. If you feel like a rat on a boring treadmill, activity seems like a bad thing. But if you are enjoying yourself, like our sweaty tennis player, the motion itself becomes part of the fun. If you are truly playing, you don't think ahead to the future; you are focused on enjoying the present. The rewards that come after the action are extra.

"Work" should not be a category separate from "play." Both are activities, and humans need stimulation to keep livng and growing. The only difference is that we usually see the immediate material goals from work. The valuable effects of play are usually more long-term. But that shouldn't cause us to focus on the result as a measure of the value of the activity. The process of earning a livelihood should also be a focus on present enjoyment, the sweat of the activity being part of the fun, and the future rewards an extra bonus.

You shouldn't feel you are violating your ethical standards by not being miserable while you work (The Work Ethic). Nor should you feel you are acting in a vacuum that has no relation to other parts of your life (The Work Mystique). You have a right to enjoy work. You have a right to find it meaningful.

Job Enrichment: Practical or Preachy?

In our terms, then, job enrichment would consist of making your job a richer experience for you. We would want to make it less profane and more sacred, so that your soul grows from the experience. We would want to make it more consistent with your ideals for a good life. Is this an unrealistic expectation? If not, how do we accomplish this goal?

We can do this by using the concept of religion as something that ties together the parts of your life and gives them meaning. In Chapter Three, we'll be asking questions from a sapient perspective. Once you have begun to understand what you want from life, you can begin to plan ahead for a meaningful consistency in all aspects, including at the workplace. We can explore available techniques and methods for putting your plan into practice.

Bear with the questions that follow. Answer them honestly and write down the answers so that you can review them later. That way, you won't be tempted to give quick, superficial responses. Give yourself time to review the self-knowledge you obtain.

What else do you need to bring to this project? A desire for a more fulfilling life, a willingness to be honest with yourself, and the effort it will take to keep experimenting with alternatives. If you're suffering from soul-sickness, take heart. We're about to embark on a recovery program!

3

A Greenhouse
for People to Grow in

In Chapter Two, we looked at the ways in which the Seven Deadly Vices are affecting our worklife. Boredom, inefficiency, and lack of meaning are sickening our souls each day. How then do we change the atmosphere in the workplace? How can we do something to help ourselves, let alone those we work with?

This chapter addresses these very questions. There are actions you can take to begin to have an impact. But in order for these actions to be effective, your motivation must be clear. The questions in this chapter will help you clarify what you really need from your present situation and what you want from your future. By uncovering your needs, you can plan ahead to build meaning into your future.

How do we decide what we need from life? Obviously, there is no one answer to this question. Everybody needs and wants different things. Furthermore, what we think we want and what is healthy for us are not always the same things. We have to accept the fact that whatever answer we make now may need to be revised. As we learn more, our needs and wants change.

Maybe the attitude with which we begin our search for the answers is more important than the actual answer. If this is to be a lifelong process of learning and growing, we need an attitude that will help us do both in a healthy way. Maybe the best way to describe an appropriate attitude would be again, to use some words you may have learned in religious training: *faith, hope,* and *charity.*

Faith means that you really commit yourself to the belief that there is meaning in your existence. It means that you want to stop living by exception and put some consistency into your actions. *Faith* means that you want to live your life to the fullest, with grace, enjoyment, and a sense of purpose.

Hope means that you really believe you can accomplish something. It means that you are willing to keep trying to change your own small corner of the world, even if you cannot change everything. Of course, we would all like to make some great grand gesture that improves the entire world. Sometimes we get discouraged with anything less.

But if the world is really interconnected, then large gestures have large consequences, and we may not be wise enough to foresee all the possible disruptions that we could cause. Perhaps it is braver and wiser to concentrate on improving our own life first. We may not get to be as famous, but we may be able to do more good that way. It is difficult to feel we are working alone and unsung, but faith and hope are more loyal companions than all the world's applause.

Charity is the third internal cornerstone for a full

life. If religion is the recognition that all living beings are connected then charity is the logical result of that recognition. *Charity* originally meant love of one's fellow creatures. Today it is too often used to mean "giving to one poorer than yourself." This later meaning destroys the value of the concept.

Charity is a consideration and kindliness towards living beings. It is based on a recognition of their relation to us, our equality as creatures with a divine spark. Being thoughtful of another person should be a mark of respect and recognition, not a chance to be patronizing or superior. Furthermore, we must include ourselves as people who deserve kindness. There are as many people who find it hard to be kind to themselves as there are people who find it hard to be kind to others.

True charity exists between these two extremes. It means caring for yourself and caring for others. Many people have the misconception that caring for yourself is selfish in a bad way. Others feel that sacrificing yourself to give to other people is stupid. If we want to be realistic we must acknowledge that going to either extreme creates negative consequences.

If you consistently deny your own feelings in order to fill other people's needs you will eventually be drained and burned-out. If you consistently fill your own needs by ignoring the feelings of others you will eventually be lonely and shallow. The best balance is achieved when your own needs are met, and you have the energy and resources to respond to the needs of the people around you. This kind of charitable attitude towards ourselves and others is vital to a smoothly functioning office. Let's look at how to use faith, hope, and charity in a practical way to revitalize our workplace.

A Practical Approach
to a Healthy Business Atmosphere

The Seven Deadly Vices pollute the workplace environment and make it impossible for people to work and grow. What we need to do is diagnose the ineffective and destructive patterns at work and apply some strategies to change the situation. We can create a greenhouse within which workers can blossom if we can encourage virtues instead of vices.

Obviously, the higher your position in your company, the more resources you have available to change these destructive patterns. But anyone can have an impact, even if it is just on their own job and no other. Like yeast in bread dough, a little portion can leaven a whole loaf. If you are happier and more productive, the effects will be contagious. People respect results, and if you sincerely improve your own attitude towards your job, others may start learning from your example.

It is especially important to realize that we can combat a feeling of meaninglessness by recognizing the importance of small everyday actions. By remembering that each little task adds to the significance of the whole day, we can begin to believe that our daily chores are matters of great consequence. Doing every task with grace results in a day that feels meaningful.

Forcing yourself to do a job that has no meaning to you poisons your soul. Tasks that have no purpose, that simply push paper around, waste your talent and your energy. It may be that there are some things you are doing that are truly wasteful and inefficient. And we are going to suggest that you take steps to eliminate these things. But there are other tasks that only seem meaningless because you have not looked for their connections with the world around you or with your own needs.

We are going to do some exercises that will help you to see the place of each small action in the greater scheme of things. Gradually, we will build up your idea of a better life, both at the workplace and at home. We will start out by asking you to be "selfish"; in other words, to focus on what you want from your job. Other people will have to ask themselves the same questions, but their answers willl all be different. We each have to experiment with our own ways of living up to our potential.

The antidote to:	*Is:*
Loss of meaning	Faith
Despair	Hope
Soul-sickness	Charity

Diagnosing Ineffective Patterns

Ask yourself the following questions and write down the answers. Let yourself answer openly and honestly. Take as much time as you need; don't cut yourself short or limit yourself to just a few words. Some people find it helps to pretend they are talking to a kind, supportive friend.

Exercise one: the here and now

These first six questions can help you look at your thoughts and feelings toward the task part of your job. Answer the following:

1. What is your job supposed to consist of?
2. How do you actually spend your time on the job?
3. What parts of your job do you enjoy most?
4. What parts of your job do you hate most?
5. What do you do best on the job?
6. Where are you weakest on the job?

Now we want to move to some questions that help us focus on how you interact with other aspects of your workplace. Complete the following sentences:

7. When things are going badly, I usually ...
8. The person I have the most trouble with on the job is ... because ...
9. My biggest problem at work is ...
10. The one thing I'd like to change about my boss is ...

It might help at this point to summarize your responses in a chart. On the left hand side of a sheet of paper, list all the activities you mentioned in response to questions one and two. Then make five columns to the right of the list. Label the columns *I Like, I Do Well, I Hate, I Do Badly,* and *Time Spent* (on that activity). Your chart should look like this:

My job

I like   I do well   I hate   I do badly   Time spent

Using your responses, write the different aspects of your job at the extreme right. These are the activities you listed when answering questions one and two. Then make a check under each heading that applies to that part of your work. In question three, you listed the task you liked; in question four, you listed the ones you dislike. In question five, you listed the tasks you do well, and in question six, the ones you think you do badly. Your answer to question two should help you figure out what percentage of time you spend on each of these jobs.

Here's a sample list that might have been prepared by a social worker:

My job

	I like	I do well	I hate	I do badly	Time spent
Visiting clients	xx	xx			15%
Driving in car		?	xx		50%
Filling out forms			xx	xx	10%
Talking with my supervisor	xx	xx			20%

Here's another example, this one from a salesclerk:

My job

	I like well	I do	I hate	I do badly	Time spent
Customer Sales	50%	xx	50%		35%
Paperwork			xx	xx	20%
Storing deliveries			xx	xx	10%
Answering questions	xx	xx			25%
Accounting			xx		10%

Notice that these examples show a common pattern. We tend to do better at the tasks we like best, and do worse at the things we dislike. The social worker put a question mark next to driving, because it seemed like a task that couldn't be done well. One either does it or not! It's hard to feel good about doing a task that seems valueless.

But even a routine task like driving could be done more effectively. The social worker could plan ahead to save time, scheduling visits that are close geographically on the same day, or checking a map for the most efficient route to travel. Too often we make a boring job longer and harder because it doesn't seem worth the effort to plan ahead. Sometimes we are so annoyed by a boring task that we ignore the possibilities.

Notice some of the same patterns in the second example from the salesclerk. This chart also reflects the tendency to do better at the tasks that are liked and to do badly at the tasks that are disliked. Notice, too, the unanswered question of how this person feels about the accounting and bookkeeping. We often ignore our skill at things we do well if they occur in a context that seems trivial or boring. But they may prove unexpected assets when we look to future improvement in our job situation.

It is also important to consider how you spend your time on the job. Some people try to avoid doing the jobs they don't like; others spend too much of their time agonizing over them. Trivial details can take up more time than they are worth, especially if you spend extra time fretting over them instead of doing them. How are you spending your valuable time? Are you using it mostly where it will have the most value? Can you think of ways to reduce the time spent on less important tasks?

Now let's move on to questions seven through ten. Again let's look for ways to improve the situation by changing either your internal attitude or the external variables. Let's be really rough on ourselves and see whether the Seven Deadly Office Vices contribute to the problem!

How do you act when things are going badly at the office (Question seven)? Does pride keep you from asking others for their help in solving the difficulties? Does greed make you fear letting others get credit for their help? Does sloth make you stop trying? Do you say to yourself: "It's not my problem; let somebody else find a solution"?

Who do you have the most trouble with on the job (Question eight)? Does cowardice make you afraid to confront your problems with this person? Does unkindness lead you to make the situation worse with your displays of hostility? Do you try to convince yourself that it's not your fault? Maybe you've been dishonest and haven't really told the other person what you dislike about their behavior. It is possible to be both honest and kind. And that's the only way for the two of you to work together on your problems.

What was your answer to question nine? Go through our list of vices and see if any of them are making the situation worse. Remember that the point of this analysis isn't to feel guilty, but to accept responsibility for your part of the problem. You may not have control over others, but you do have control over the things you do that make the problem worse.

What would you like to change most about your boss (Question ten)? Is there any behavior of yours that encourages your boss to act that way? For example, maybe you feel that your boss is too critical of you. Try to remember specific criticisms that your boss has made in the last week or so. Write them down. Now go back to the chart you prepared from questions one through six.

Were any of the complaints about things you dislike doing? Were they justified complaints? Maybe you hate paperwork and try to avoid it whenever possible. Instead of waiting until your supervisor complains, try being honest and seeing if you can work out a solution together.

Were any of the complaints about things you feel you don't do well? Again, try being honest about your fears. Maybe you can ask for more training in one of those areas. Or maybe you'd rather someone else be given the responsibility for that task.

Was that a frightening thought? Many people assume they should keep taking on responsibilities even if they don't like them or don't want them. This isn't necessarily an effective way to proceed. Think again about where you want to be in five years. Think about what you want to learn more about. There may be some tasks you really do want to learn to do better. But there may be others that you'd rather not spend your time on. Perhaps you could trade one of these unpleasant jobs for a responsibility you'd like better.

If you have trouble with the thought of being honest about your problems, if you are afraid of losing power at the office, pick up a book such as *Realistic Leadership* (Prentice-Hall, 1983). It will help you sort out your conflicts about power and responsibility. It also has tips on how to express your needs effectively to your boss and to your co-workers.

The spirit of a healthy workplace is a collaborative one. People have to work together to accomplish a task efficiently. You can improve your own ability to fill your needs and your company's goals at the same time. First you have to examine your goals carefully. Then you need to understand the obstacles that get in the way of obtaining those goals. Finally, you have to be willing to change the behaviors you have that help create those obstacles. It isn't easy, but the rewards are worth the effort.

The examples given are relatively brief, but they illustrate the process of gathering information about yourself and analyzing that information. Refer back to your chart. Try to relate it to the information in the other questions. Think of yourself as a detective, trying to put some consistency into your career. The more specific you are about the information you list, the more useful it will be to you as we continue with our exercises.

Exercise two: the future

Taking a fresh sheet of paper, complete the following sentences with the first thought that enters your mind. Don't discard any idea; explore the possibilities fully.

11. In five years, I'd like to be ...
12. I'd really like to learn more about ...
13. Of all the jobs I ever had, the one(s) I enjoyed most was/ were ..., because ...
14. I want to become the kind of person who ...
15. I'd prefer to work in a workplace where ...

Examine your answers to these five questions. List all the specific factors that went into each response. For example, suppose you said that in five years, you'd like to be district sales manager. Why do you feel that way? What appeals to you about the job? You might list the following factors:

- More money!
- I wouldn't have to report to Fred Smith anymore. He's

always pushing me to sell more, even if it means more time on the road.

- I don't want to be a salesman all my life; I ought to move up in the company.

Let's look carefully at these responses, because they can help you to sort out your real priorities. "More money" is a common response, but have you considered the following: How much more money? Enough to pay bills? Or enough to be able to brag about? Sometimes we want more money because it represents an achievement, something to measure our success, not because we need more to live on. Your second item suggests you don't get much positive feedback. Your third item suggests that you want more recognition for your work. Is it really money alone that you want, or does it just represent status and approval?

Maybe you want the extra money so you can spend it on hobbies and family outings. Maybe it represents more free time to you. The second item on your list suggests that you feel you have to put in too many hours on the job. But if recreation is what you really want, will the job of district sales manager allow you the time to enjoy the extra money?

Do you see now why it is important to start with your needs and work from there? Too often we say we want what we're "supposed" to want, instead of really caring about what we do want. Did you answer "district sales manager" because that was "supposed" to be the next step up? Examine your needs again carefully. Is that really the job you want in five years? Will it involve extra pressure and more time? Will that satisfy your real desires for recognition, a feeling of accomplishment and more time for recreation? Or will it make you feel more pressured, more frustrated, and less relaxed? Think about it!

Suppose we thought about other ways to satisfy your real needs. There are many other alternative ways to improve your situation. Is there a way to make Fred Smith aware of your need for more positive feedback? Chapter Five will explore the best ways to communicate with other people, without being either bully or victim.)

Can you adjust your internal attitudes so that you are less upset by his poor management? In later chapters, we'll continue looking at ways to create more balance in your life. If you feel good about yourself you are less likely to be affected by the stupid or thoughtless people in this world. If a change in your internal feelings isn't sufficient to improve the situation, can you transfer to a new district, or even a new job, where your supervisor is less of a problem?

The important thing to remember is that if you blindly head for a goal without examining it carefully, you may find yourself no happier than you are now. If you think you want something, look carefully at the things about it that appeal to you. Maybe there are other ways to fill those needs. Maybe the things you thought you wanted wouldn't satisfy those needs after all. It pays to check it out!

Now let's move along and look at some possible responses to question twelve. What would you like to learn more about and why? Here are some responses that might be listed by an assembler in a factory:

- I'd like to know more about the "big picture," what the finished product does and how it works.
- I'd like a chance to learn a job where people cared what I did; I feel lost here.

- This is silly, but I usually feel stupid next to the office workers; I wish I could learn to be comfortable talking to them.

Some people might jump to the "obvious" ways to meet these desires, like getting a better job or going back to school. But both of these solutions take a long time before results are achieved. Furthermore, they may be impractical if the assembler's finances or work experiences don't provide enough resources. Remember, we're starting with your needs and looking for alternative ways of filling those needs. If your needs are met now, if you are happy now, you can make better choices about your future.

For example, the second and third items might be filled by offering to help a local community theatre group. Extra hands are always needed, and it provides a good free education in public speaking, becoming comfortable in different roles, and exposure to both classic and current literature. Stage hands are appreciated by the cast and the audience, for their work is essential. A few small parts in a play may provide a taste of applause and recognition and contribute to an overall feeling of pride.

Back at the factory, these experiences might lead to an improved ability to communicate with others and more self-confidence in approaching those in authority. Our assembler might then decide to act on item one on his list. Many companies are delighted to have employees who want to learn more about how the whole process works. They are often willing to rotate workers so they can learn several different jobs, thus increasing their value to the company.

At this point, it might be appropriate to take evening courses in areas related to the job. (A workshop on

Quality Circles, for example, is valuable for workers in production.) Most companies have educational reimbursement programs that help defray the cost of school expenses.

This is only one possible alternative, but notice how much it accomplishes. It immediately starts filling some of the worker's needs, while providing the groundwork for both short-term and long-term advancement. And it is based on that individual's specific desires, strengths, and weaknesses.

The same analysis can be done with your other responses. Question thirteen reminded you of jobs that you enjoyed in the past. Can you use those memories to focus on the factors that you would like from all jobs?

Question fourteen was designed to make you think about the kind of person you would like to be. What factors in your current job encourage you to be that way? Which discourage you?

Using this information about yourself, think about ways of putting more of what you want into your job. Take question fifteen. What can you do to create the kind of work environment that you would like to see? Friendly, creative, cooperative? What can you do to encourage this kind of atmosphere? Don't leave it up to others!

You can start by eliminating the things you do that discourage or counteract the atmosphere you want. Look closely at the people and tasks that cause you problems at your job. Then evaluate your own contribution to the situation. Don't respond to hostility with hostility or to apathy with apathy. Take the initiative; don't just passively send back the same attitudes you are complaining about.

Maybe our discussion of the Seven Deadly Vices

seems old-fashioned to you. But it certainly puts a new perspective on typical workplace behavior! It's worth taking an "old-fashioned" look if you start having second thoughts about the way you've been handling problems on the job. Think about problems *before* you have to deal with them! Only if you plan ahead will you be able to handle situations in a healthy and consistent manner.

We need to look at one other area in which people fail to make the connections they need to feel good about their work. Do you know how your job fits into the larger scheme of things? Understanding how your job fits into your company's purpose and how your company fits into your society as a whole is important in feeling good about yourself.

Nowadays, some people choose their jobs on the basis of this kind of connection. They choose jobs in solar energy or health services partly because they like what those jobs do for our society. But sometimes people in traditional office or manufacturing jobs haven't bothered to explore their relationship to the country as a whole.

Find out more about how your particular job contributes to the smooth functioning of your company. Then find out more about what your company does. Use the library and other resources to gather information about how and why your company is useful to the economy. Find out more about the history of how your industry got started. What needs does it fill? How does it help people? What does it provide? What would be the impact if your company's product or service ceased to exist?

You may find this research quite exciting. It may surprise you to find out how much impact you have on modern society. Maybe you will find out things that bother you too. You will have to decide how to handle this information. Maybe you can make suggestions that will improve something. Maybe you will find out that you are not comfortable in the industry in which you are now working (although this is rather unlikely). But now you will have the information to help you make a meaningful connection between your job and the "real world."

I have lost at least one job because I insisted on living up to the industry safety standards after I learned their importance. And I annoyed some important people in another company when I learned enough to point out that we were wasting several thousand dollars each week in inappropriate computer design. In each case, though, it was worth it to me to know that I was doing the most meaningful job possible.

We all have to live with ourselves first. Each day we look at our own faces in the mirror. In order to like and be proud of the person we see, we sometimes have to go back to basics. We have to ask ourselves some simple questions. What do I want out of life? Why is my job important to the world? How do I fit into the greater scheme of things? How can I be the person I want to be?

Sometimes we simply forget to ask these questions of ourselves. Or we puzzle over the questions, but don't bother to systematically evaluate our thoughts. The exercises in this chapter are a way of granting permission to yourself to ask these simple questions and a way of acknowledging their value in setting your personal goals.

But these exercises will only help if you take the time to think about how to use the information. Knowing what you want is of little value if you don't start planning ways to get it. If tomorrow you take a step, however small, toward your goals, you are that much closer to reaching them.

Remember, too, that these exercises need to be

repeated. You need to ask yourself the same basic questions periodically and revise your plans accordingly. We change and grow every day of our lives. We can't expect our goals to stay exactly the same. By reviewing your needs and plans every so often, you won't slip accidentally into an outmoded and irrelevant existence.

Keep yourself on target. Adjust your aim from time to time. Keep faith in your dreams. Be hopeful about what you can accomplish. And grant yourself the charity to accept that even if you don't reach your goals, you grow by trying for them!

4

Polishing the Tarnish on the Golden Rule

There's a very popular cartoon in the workplace today. You'll find it on posters, ashtrays, everywhere! Next to a picture of a toadstool is the caption: "I must be a mushroom, 'cause they keep me in the dark and feed me bullshit!" Since this shows up in so many places, it must express a pretty common feeling among workers.

When Did the Truth Become Unrealistic?

More information is withheld from workers than is given to them. One might think that businesses had decided that truth was impractical in the workplace! Too often managers weaken their workforce by keeping information in the hands of a few at the top rather than passing it along to the workers. This tendency permeates all aspects of business.

For example, we spend very little time training people when we first hire them. In Japan, companies train workers an average of 200 days per ten years of work. Contrast that with our American average of 20 days of training per ten years of work.

Then we make very little effort to let workers know where they fit in once they're on the job. It's almost like a conspiracy to keep workers from learning to do their jobs well! Many companies don't bother to give the employee an up-to-date job description. Many managers never comment on the employee's performance unless something goes wrong.

The worst part of this conspiracy of misinformation is the infamous yearly review (sometimes held twice yearly). This is usually a nerve-wracking experience that conveys too little information too late to be of any use in improving job performance. Most often this kind of review seems instituted to provide upper management with an excuse for not giving a fair salary raise. They say they won't give a raise for poor performance, yet they avoided helping the employee to learn to perform well.

There might very well be real reasons for not raising the employee's salary to meet rising costs. These reasons might range from insufficient profit to greedy owners. But rather than explain these reasons to the worker, management often chooses to give the employee a "guilt trip" by pretending the employee has not done a good enough job.

If you stop to look logically at this chain of reasoning, you realize how illogical it really is. Either someone is doing a good enough job to deserve a living wage or they aren't. If they are not doing a good enough job, you either teach them to do it well or you ask them to leave. Giving a five percent raise when food prices have gone up fifteen percent, makes no sense at all. Either the salary is based on realistic figures or it isn't realistic!

In some types of business, it may seem encouraging to award a bonus to workers who are outstanding in their department. Unfortunately, if you reward only the best in each department, you encourage competition between employees rather than cooperation for the good of the company. And then there are those jobs whose output is hard to measure. Presumably every job in your company is important to the survival of that company. A person who performs that necessary job shouldn't be cheated out of a living wage.

The bottom line is lack of communication. Some companies would cringe at the thought of showing workers the company bookkeeping and explaining that there wasn't enough of a profit to pay all workers the salary they need to live on. Nor would companies explain that there was enough profit, but top management would rather take the extra instead of raising the overall wages.

Other managers will shrug their shoulders and explain that a particular employee didn't "deserve" a raise this year. They make this judgment on an individual who still has to cope with inflation and rising costs. These same managers are usually the ones who don't bother to take the time on a daily basis to help that employee learn to do the job better. Yet they would be greatly upset if someone said they didn't deserve to get a manager's salary since they couldn't train their employees properly!

In *Realistic Leadership*, published by Prentice-Hall, I elaborated on the role of managers in collaborative leadership. Like this book, *Realistic Leadership* addresses the need to be honest with yourself as well as with others. Often when people explore their motivations for withholding information, they find their actions based on emotional hang-ups rather than practical logic.

For example, suppose you believe that everyone at your office is out to steal your job. If you think knowledge equals power, you may be afraid to share that power with anyone else. You may find yourself keeping necessary information from your subordinates because of your own insecurity. By creating an atmosphere of mistrust and inefficiency, you may end up losing the very job you tried to protect.

When you do this, you show a lack of respect for the people around you. But worse yet, you show lack of respect for yourself. No one else can really take a job away from you unless they are downright dishonest. And gaining anything by dishonesty is a very precarious position to be in. People who steal or lie always have to worry about getting caught. They can lose everything they gained and destroy all future credibility if their dishonesty is uncovered. And it always is! Keep your job safe by being honest and by encouraging teamwork and a supportive atmosphere. Give yourself the respect you deserve by believing in yourself. Don't hide behind a false front.

It is important to realize that your general attitudes about people and life affect the way you act in the workplace. As we discussed in Chapter One, people often pretend that different rules apply in different situations. The result is a life that is disconnected and unsatisfying. The more you can integrate all the parts of your life into a consistent whole, the more satisfying your life becomes.

It is very difficult to get a sense of connectedness when half the picture is missing. Nothing is more frustrating than trying to put a jigsaw puzzle together when someone has removed half the pieces. When you refuse to examine your hidden motives, you are hiding half of your feelings from yourself. If you hide half of your feelings from yourself, your actions will be inconsistent and petty. If you hide half of the relevant information from co-workers, their task will be frustrating and exhausting.

Respect and Responsibility

We're faced with a paradox: Treating people with respect means treating yourself with respect as well. Open communication with others means that you have to be in open communication with yourself. The golden rule takes on a new aspect. It was never meant as an injunction to not be respectful of yourself. It does mean that if you don't treat yourself well, you won't know how to treat others well.

This golden rule is found in many forms, in nearly every religious movement the world over. Let's look at the many ways in which this advice has been expressed and then discuss its implications.

From the Christian Sermon on the Mount: "All things whatsoever ye would that men should do to you, do ye even so to them."

From the Hindu Mahabharata: "This is the true rule of life and the sum of duty: do nothing unto others which might cause you pain if it were done to you. Guard and do by the things of others as they would do by their own."

From the Buddhist Udana-Varga: "Do not hurt others in any way that you would find hurtful. Seek for others the happiness you desire for yourself."

From the Confucian Analects: "Is there one word of counsel by which one should act throughout his whole life? It is indeed loving kindness; do not unto others what you would not have them do unto you."

From the Taoist T'ai Shang Kan Ying P'ien: "Consider your neighbor's gain as your own, and your neighbor's loss as your own."

From the Jewish Talmud: "What is hateful to you, do not do to your fellow man. That is the entire Law; all the rest is Commentary."

From the Zoroastrian Dadistan-i-dinik: "Only that nature can be considered good which refuses to do unto another what is not good for itself. Do as you would be done by."

From the Islamic Sunna: "Let none of you treat his brother in a way he himself would not like to be treated."

From the writings of the Roman Stoics: "The law imprinted on the hearts of all men is to love the members of society as themselves."

From the ancient Greek: "Do not that to a neighbor which you would take ill from him."

The overwhelming message is the need to recognize the connections between ourselves and others. All religions and philosophies encourage a recognition of the close relationship among all people. If this is true, then the golden rule is more than just good social advice, it is a very practical warning to ourselves. We cannot hurt another without hurting ourselves as well.

If you want a mystical truth revealed to you, consider this: Each time we hurt another human being, we lose a part of ourself. This is the hidden corollary of the golden rule. What we do unto others, we do to ourselves. When we lie to others, we lose the Truth. When we hurt others, we encourage pain. When we deny our responsibility, we suffer the consequences. When we act out of malice, it is we who harden our hearts and lose our souls.

Some people refer to this as the Law of Karma. Psychoanalysts would talk about the psychodynamics you set up. Behaviorists would talk about what stimulus you create to encourage a negative response. Transactional analysts would talk about the games you play and the negative strokes you get as a payoff.

It doesn't matter what you call it. It happens, whatever name you use. You are being impractical and unrealistic if you think you can avoid the negative effects of negative actions. You are responsible for your behavior. There is nowhere you can hide to avoid the consequences of it. The reason folklore says that "The road to hell is paved with good intentions" is that your motivations don't usually affect the results. You might as well acknowledge that everything you do has an impact on the future, and plan now to make sure the impact is positive.

Most people don't hurt others out of malice; they are destructive because they are not treating themselves well. If we are afraid of conflict, we are likely to hide our problems from others. Whether we do this at the office or at home, we end up lying to ourselves as well as others. The result is a crisis that affects all of us. Others get hurt because we were lying to ourselves.

If we are greedy, it is because we are not happy with the way our lives are. The pain we inflict on others stems from our own dissatisfaction. If we lust for sex or power and manipulate others in our efforts to get these things, it is because we don't know how to ask for what we want directly. We may feel we have to sneak around to get what we want because we don't deserve to have our needs met.

We may put others down because we are insecure about our own self-esteem. We may act out of prejudice because we distrust our own ability to think things through and make a logical decision. In short, most of the misery we inflict on other human beings stems directly from our own misery with ourselves. Learning to treat yourself well makes it easier to treat others well. Feeling good about yourself tends to make you want to share that feeling with others, rather than begrudge them that pleasure.

Part of the problem is ignorance. We are often so wrapped up in our own misery that we don't take the time to look at the consequences of our actions. Maybe religion has to be important to us before we bother to take notice of the effects of what we do. If we really have faith, the belief that we are connected to the world and to the divine, then we recognize that none of our actions are unimportant.

Many people are frightened by faith. They don't want to be important because they don't want to feel responsible for their actions. They see responsibility only in terms of blame. This is one of the great failures of organized religion, the fact that so often it encourages guilt. Harping on sin and punishment seems, to me, to be a waste of time and energy. Every action has its consequences; that's a natural law. But people can be so paralyzed by guilt that they cope badly with these consequences and make things even worse. Guilt has done more to destroy religious feeling than any other human emotion. It makes people afraid of faith, kills their hope, and distracts them from real charity.

Taking responsibility for your life doesn't mean feeling guilty because you're not perfect! It means realizing that you can take the initiative in changing your life for the better! Getting rid of guilt can leave you free to accept faith that you have a place in the cosmic scheme of things. Getting rid of guilt means you can concentrate on the hope that lets you believe you can make things better. And it means you can treat both yourself and others with the respectful charity that all humans deserve from each other.

You can even extend the concept of charity beyond your immediate social sphere if you are really in touch with the basic meaning of religion, that sense of all things being related by the Divinity. You can begin to recognize that you are hurting yourself when you pollute the atmosphere, misuse natural resources, or needlessly kill other living beings. The knowledge we have gotten from science is useful, but without the wisdom of a religious perspective, we are in grave danger of acting irresponsibly. The ultimate sin may be the destruction of ourselves and our planet, but by that time it will be too late for talk of guilt. It is better to talk of responsibility now, than to complain about guilt later on!

Peer Pressure and the Need to Be Accepted

Many people insist on shirking responsibility for their own lives by putting the burden on others. Instead of learning more about what their own conscience says, they keep trying to live up to what they think others expect of them. They substitute the knowledge of statistics for the wisdom of their soul!

One of the most misused words I know of is the word normal. Most people use it as though it referred to an objective reality. Worse yet, they act as though being "normal" equalled being healthy. When people walk into a doctor's office and ask "Am I normal?" they are really asking for a judgment on whether they are sane and whole.

But that assessment cannot be made on the basis of

the statistical norm. Should we compare ourselves to the people around us or the national norms or to some other group? Futhermore, just because many people are doing something, it does not mean it is healthy for them, for you, and for humans in general. Being different from the people around you is a reflection of differences in experience, knowledge, and beliefs. You can't base questions of health or sanity on a simple statistical standard.

You may cringe every time someone raises their voice to you. Perhaps when you were a child, you developed this defense against being struck by an angry parent. It has become a habit that you don't even think about. Someone yells, and you react in the only way you have learned. This does not make you crazy. However, it is not necessarily a useful way of dealing with loud voices. It may make it difficult for you to achieve your goals in an argument or stand up for what you believe in. After all, as soon as your opponent shouts, you act like a frightened child.

Suppose you have grown enough to realize that you are an adult. Suppose you decide you deserve the same respect as any other human being. And suppose you realize that your old pattern is having a negative effect on your relationships with other people. Your new feelings of self-like plus your motivation to improve how you relate to people may lead you to change. By consciously practicing new behaviors, you can break the old habit and develop a new style of coping with loud voices.

Now imagine what would happen if many people around you tended to cringe when yelled at. In other words, it was normal to act like a child and back down in that situation. You might choose to continue cringing even if it hurt your feelings of self-esteem, even if it created less than satisfactory relationships, even if you knew it was illogical, all because you were afraid of social disapproval. Or you could try to act healthier and accept the fact that you would then be different from most people around you.

It's not an easy choice. But many people in every generation have had to make it. If women are expected to cringe before angry men, then women have had to face that choice. If blacks are expected to cringe before angry whites, then blacks have had to face that choice. Whatever your ethnic background, gender, or religion, somewhere in human culture you might have had to make the choice between what is healthy and what is normal.

This becomes part of what I consider the religious element in any life. This is where the wisdom that recognizes connectedness becomes important. Should you behave in a manner that is statistically normal in order to fit better into society? If you do that, your behavior is likely to hurt your self-respect and destroy your belief in the spark of divinity within you. If everyone did this, then the status quo would never change. Trying to be normal can insure that nothing is done that builds upon your beliefs and makes them become reality.

Should you challenge the normal expected behavior and risk the consequences? You may feel very alone, you may risk economic loss, you may even be physically hurt or killed. You may be risking destruction without any guarantee of being able to change anything. Yet if no one ever tries the unexpected, society might never change. Can suffering accomplish nothing, yet still mean something?

Or should you try to be practical, complying outwardly when necessary but looking for ways to affect change without risk? You can run the danger of hating yourself when you comply and feeling futile when you don't make a meaningful impact. Or you may even get so lost in playing the role of acceptance that you stop believing in your own self-worth.

There is no one right decision, only many difficult choices. The situation is not hopeless. Obviously social changes occur, and we all contribute to them in some way. The point is that it is an individual decision, a religious decision if you will. You must decide what creates the most connectedness in your life. You must find the combination of actions that will allow you to feel good about yourself and good about the world. All aspects of being Homo sapiens must be considered equally. This integration is the heart of religion and the soul of an individual.

Practical ethics must be weighed, and the impact on other people considered. Your feelings of hope and fear must be taken into account. Physical abilities and limitations have an impact. Mind, heart, and body must be integrated into a blueprint that is the source of consistent behavior. And from this integration arises that miraculous and unmeasurable aspect of humanity: a sapient soul.

Perhaps you are saying to yourself: "But if I was in a situation that clear-cut, I wouldn't have any trouble feeling religious. It's the petty routine of everyday life that kills my soul." The idea behind this book is that careful thinking about your own life can make your personal consistency more clear to you. Don't wait until you are forced by a crisis to integrate yourself. You can choose to become sapient now!

Bigotry and Prejudice:
Sins Against the Economy

If someone told you that you were doing something that was unethical, cruel, and destructive to your own economic well being, you'd be shocked. You couldn't imagine consciously doing something that had negative effects on so many levels. Yet unconscious prejudice is the most common and most insidious poison in our society today.

Prejudice means to prejudge something; to form an opinion without taking the care or the time to be fair. Every time we make an assumption about another human being, we are automatically not being fair. If our assumption about that person is a positive one, we are not likely to do them harm (although it can lead us to be hurtful to others if we exclude them on the basis of our positive assumptions about one person.)

But if our assumption about another person is negative, we are hurting another person unfairly. Given the way in which self-fulfilling prophecies work, we are even likely to act in ways which encourage this negative assumption to come true. We do nothing to change our world for the better, and we needlessly hurt ourselves and others.

Furthermore, in business, prejudice has a serious economic effect. You hurt your company by limiting potential workers. If you eliminate job applicants because of irrelevant factors (like their gender, race, or age), you are denying your company a chance to choose from all qualified possibilities. You may miss the best person for the job because you acted with without thinking about your real needs! Making assumptions about what a person can do, without knowing the relevant facts, is a senseless waste of the most valuable resource: people.

Multiply this waste by the number of decisions made each day in this country, and you begin to see the drastic economic impact. For example, we assume women shouldn't work, so we fail to offer them sufficient job opportunities. We especially discriminate against working mothers, so we fail to encourage adequate and inexpensive day-care facilities. Women are still paid less on the national average than men, so they may not be able to afford the cost of private day care, even when available. We have created a nationally destructive situation. Millions of women are faced with the choice of adding to the nation's welfare burden or struggling to stay out of poverty in unrewarding jobs.

We discriminate against working fathers by ignoring the importance of their relationships with their families. We discourage them from spending time with infants, generally, by penalizing them for trying to take a leave of absence when a child is born. We force men to bear an unequal share of the financial responsibilities by discouraging women from working productively. If a man happens to be a single parent, he begins to face the choices that most women have to struggle with daily.

It is an unpleasant situation but not without hope. Women and men who recognize the importance of a well balanced life are creating their own methods of coping. Flexible working schedules, company-run day care centers, jobs that can be split between two people—these are some of the alternatives developed by people who took the initiative to improve their world. By doing so, they are improving the economy as well. But it is still an uphill struggle.

Why do so many people choose to stifle potential

instead of encourage growth and flexibility? It isn't logical, it isn't practical, and it isn't economically sound. We are wasting human potential, then complaining about the results. We refuse to respect the spark of divinity in all humanity, then we wonder why soul-sickness is reaching epidemic proportions. The answer is clear.

Gender-role prejudice is only one form of discrimination. We discriminate against people because of their ethnic background, their religious affiliation, their age, even the clothes they wear or the way they cut their hair. What foolishness! Instead of valuing the richness that results from a diversity of experience, we violate the essence of religion by denying our connection with other humans. Our bigotry creates the kind of world we all deplore, one filled with hate, dishonesty, envy, and despair. What kind of world could we create if we acted only with respect instead of prejudice?

When we act on irrational prejudices, we are denying religion. Instead of recognizing our responsibility to the world with which we are connected, we negate our impact by perpetuating waste and destructiveness. Instead of admiring the miracle of human variety, we refuse to respect anyone different from ourselves. We give lip service to the concept that God is infinitely complex, and that we are made in God's image. If we believe that, then we must face the fact that prejudice and bigotry are acts of disrespect toward the Divine.

The irony of this is that the most bigoted people are often the unhappiest. They take their own fears and insecurities and twist them into disrespect toward others. It's too bad they can't learn to treat themselves with charity. If they were happy with themselves and leading well-balanced lives, they would feel free to think logically about the consequences of their actions. Instead of turning their backs on religion, they might be able to appreciate the way human differences manifest the infinity of the Ultimate Source.

Why Charity Begins at Home

Unless you feel good about yourself, it's hard to feel charitable toward other people. If you don't practice honesty and fairness with yourself, you won't know how to give it to others. In Chapter Five, we'll examine what we expect of other people and examine specific ways to treat them better. Maybe there are some guidelines we can apply that will help others as well as ourselves.

Then we'll return to this issue of ways to do well unto ourselves. Understanding ourselves better is important if religion is to have any relevance to our daily lives, for religion should be active, not passive. It is the act of seeing the meaning in everyday events. It takes an effort. It requires something of us.

Grace is something we can learn. Living grace-fully requires that we open our eyes and our minds. Grace is a two way street. It is not given automatically to those unwilling to cope with it. If you don't want to feel that God is bored to "death," then let the presence of God within you wake up. Take an active role in your own life and trust in the consequences!

5
Thy Fellow People

We've been looking at your attitudes toward other people and toward yourself. We have been trying to understand the connections between ourselves and others. Now we need to probe more deeply into the specifics of what you expect from people and how you treat them.

We live in a very lonely time. Many people today feel that they are struggling alone in a callous and uncaring world. You often hear statements like, "It's a dog eat dog world" or "Nobody gives a damn anymore." Gone are the days when people got together to raise a barn or help with plowing. Today we may have one set of people we see only at our jobs and another set we see only socially. We may live in a place where we do not even know our neighbors. Going out for a drink often substitutes for sharing more meaningful time with other people.

Part of the problem is caused by our mobility and our diversity. We don't necessarily stay in the same town we were raised in; we often move to a place that is strange to us. And no matter where you live, there are more choices than ever available today about what to wear, what to do, what to think. We are all exposed to countless images and ideas. Radio, television, books, movies, newspapers, all the information we receive makes it possible for us to be more unique individuals than ever before.

We fight very hard for our personal liberty to make choices. It is perhaps one of the finest aspects of our society. But we fail to recognize the fact that we must then work extra hard to bridge those differences, so that we can still relate to other people on the basic level of friendship. Independence is a blessing, but if it makes us forget our basic dependence upon one another, it can cause loneliness.

It would be a mistake to think that if everybody thought the same way, we would be better friends. Diversity and individuality give texture and richness to our world. But sometimes we need to take our differences into consideration if we are to build bridges between people. I have visited countries where I understood little or none of the language, but when I nursed my infant or shared native food, I often found delight in the friendly reactions of the people around me. You can always find something in common with another human being.

The phrase "meaningful relationship" has become a cliché these days. The phrase itself expresses our desire for intimacy. The frequency and disdain with which it is used often expresses our frustration at not knowing how to put meaning into our communication with other people. But there are things we can do to establish this kind of close and honest bond betwen people.

First, we can acknowledge that not everyone will share our values, likes, and dislikes, and learn to enjoy them for their individuality. No one will be a carbon copy of ourself. Most people will be more different from us than they will be alike. That can be a source of learning and growth if you let it be.

Second, we can find ways to enhance the basic human bonds between us. Whether we are with friends or strangers, we can find ways to be human together. We can share some basic needs and experiences and help communication to run more smoothly on any level. In practical terms, any relationship can be improved, and new friendships can always be developed.

One of the most common complaints I hear from people in therapy is that they are lonely. Couples complain of a lack of intimacy between them. Single people complain that they don't have anyone to talk to. Men and women complain that an active social live can still leave you without friends of the opposite sex.

If any of these sound like your complaints, take heart. We're about to explore what people really want from each other. We'll try to develop some realistic guidelines for giving and getting what you want from relationships. Let's start with the question:

What Does It Take to Be Your Friend?

Have you ever thought about why you consider some people friends? What do they do that is different from other people? This is not an easy question. I'll warn you in advance that we are going to examine carefully what friendship means to you. You may end up deciding that you don't really have any close friends or that you haven't always been a good friend to others. That can be a painful realization.

On the other hand, if you understand what you want from other people, you have a better chance of having and being a good friend. So don't despair if your current relationships don't match up. Facing your expectations honestly is the best way to learn how to develop close friendships in the future. And it's the best way to improve the relationships you already have.

Think about the time you have spent with people, outside of a business context, in the last month. Did you feel satisfied with the quality of the time, or did you feel like something was missing? Did you feel like you knew them better after the evening was over or that the conversation consisted of meaningless small talk? Did you feel that they understood who you were and liked you better for it, or did you feel afraid to reveal your true self to them?

Are you seeing these people out of habit, rather than affection? Sometimes we continue to see people we are familiar with, even though we grow no closer. Or we drift into seeing people not because they are emotionally close, but because they are geographically close. Like a river, relationships need to continue to flow or they become stagnant. Relationships that do not grow may become security blankets. They may keep us from actively seeking out new friends who may encourage us to grow more.

This is not a criticism of old friends. People we have been close to for a long time may provide support for our changes. But so often people stick with "friends" (or lovers or spouses) who are no longer close because they are afraid of being alone. Inert relationships may provide a feeling of familiarity and security. But if all your current relationships have stopped growing, you may be paying too high a price for that security.

If you are unsatisfied with the quality of time spent with other people socially, check your reasons for seeing those particular people. Friends are people who get together to fill mutual emotional needs. If you are seeing people only because "it's good for business," "we've always gone out with them," or "they're nearby," you may wish to reevaluate these relationships.

If your emotional needs are not being met, take steps to improve the situation. Move beyond small talk and share a real part of yourself. Some of your current relationships may be capable of growth, if you put some effort into them. Make time to actively pursue new friendships. Don't get into the rut of sticking with what's safe and convenient.

Give yourself permission to see less of people who don't want to grow or who avoid sharing their feelings sincerely. I have learned to give up on people who respond to any emotional expression by saying "Aw, don't hassle me." or "Don't be so intense." This often signals a desire to avoid closeness in interpersonal relationships.

And don't overlook your own share of the responsibility in avoiding real closeness. So often we create the responses from people that we are afraid of. If we are paranoid and suspicious of other people, we interpret their every action as threatening. We discount any positive signs we get from them and refuse to see anything but potential danger.

People respond to this kind of suspicion by being hurt or angry. They may stop caring about our feelings in self-defense or even want to hurt us in revenge. This reinforces our original fear and creates a vicious cycle.

We feel alone and threatened. The sad part is that we are blaming other people for what we have set up.

This kind of self-fulfilling prophecy can also work in a positive direction. If we believe people are basically good, we will treat them well, without suspicion. They will be likely to act according to our expectations, thus reinforcing our positive feelings. We will tend to make excuses for the occasions when they disappoint us and give extra significance to the times when they help us. Once this cycle is set up, we will feel that we are living in a friendly and supportive world.

In both these cases, actual events are less important than our attitudes. They are less important because (1) the events are likely to be shaped by our expectations; and (2) we will give different weight to events which match our expectations. Take the initiative in examining what you think about other people and what kind of world we would like to live in. Then start believing in that kind of world, and you will have some control in creating it.

If we give kindness, we are more likely to receive it. If we trust, we are more likely to be trusted. If we open up to our friends, they are more likely to open up to us. For that reason, it may be more practical to examine what we are willing to do to *be* a friend before we criticize others. Maybe we have made it hard for our acquaintances to become the kind of friends we would like.

Fair Play Is Practical Planning

Being fair to our friends is a very practical way of learning to be happier with ourselves. If we can develop a tolerance for others based on respect and realism, we can often extend that to a fairer attitude towards ourselves. Furthermore, if we are fair to others, we are more likely to encourage them to be fair to us. We discussed above how we create by our expectations. That encourages certain behaviors from people around us. In other words, we get back from people what we give to them. How do we learn to give them what we need for ourselves? How do we learn to apply the golden rule in a practical way?

Developing tolerance towards others is an important step. We're talking about a positive acceptance of their individual characteristics, not a grudging resignation of them. We sometimes use the word *tolerance* in a negative way to indicate something we put up with because we can't or won't change it. We are using it here to refer to an active state of appreciation. We can love our family members, both because of and in spite of their differences from us. That is an active, positive kind of tolerance. Perhaps you might prefer to think of a word like *agape*, the Christian concept of love and tolerance, since it has a more positive meaning.

The first thing to remember when you are developing agape/tolerance is that faults and virtues are usually two sides of the same coin. Suppose we have a quiet friend who doesn't say much but listens well. If we need someone to pour out our heart to, we may find this person's company very helpful. We can dominate the conversation and feel that we are getting support from having an attentive listener. This person may be unlikely to reveal our feelings to anyone else, so we may feel safe in confiding our secrets.

However, on another occasion, we may inadvertently offend this same quiet person. Since our friend doesn't say much, he or she may express the anger by not visiting us for a few months. If we have the curiosity to ask why, we may or may not be told of the incident which provoked this response. We may ourselves become angry. After all, our friend "should" have told us the problem, instead of punishing us for our unintended offense. What kind of friend would do a thing like that, we ask ourselves!

If we stop to look closely at these situations, we realize that we are blaming our friend for being consistent! The characteristic tendency to avoid talking is something we admire as a virtue in one case, yet it is something we detest as a fault in another case. Our feelings toward our friend are based not on her or his nature, but on our own needs of the moment! Seems a bit unfair, doesn't it?

We can think of many other examples of blaming our friends for being who they are. We may invite friends over because they are usually the life of the party, while criticizing them at other times for being too wild. We may admire friends who are successful in their career, while criticizing them for being too pushy in social situations. In every case, we are refusing to accept that the same behavior can be a virtue in one situation and a fault in another.

While it might seem nice if all of us knew exactly when to talk and when to be quiet, when to be exciting and when to be calming, when to take the initiative and when to be laid back, it just isn't the way people are. We are all different. We all tend toward certain behavior patterns regardless of the situation. Presumably we are all trying to learn to be more balanced, but until we reach perfection (an unlikely goal in one lifetime!) we need to be accepted for who we are.

Givers, Takers, and How to
Avoid Being a Vampire

Being tolerant of your friends doesn't mean being taken advantage of by them. Nor does it mean using their traits solely for your advantage. You don't have to be a victim who feeds everyone else's needs at the expense of your own, nor a vampire who drains others with unreasonable demands. Learning to give and take in fair amounts is the essence of good relationships with other people.

Many people give because they feel they have to. They feel guilty if they say "No, I'm too busy right now." They are always putting aside their own needs, then ending up feeling resentful. This not only shows their lack of respect for themselves, it also deprives their friends of a chance to learn tolerance.

If this is your problem, get in touch with your own feelings. Before you automatically say "Yes" to someone else's demand, ask yourself "Do I really have the time and energy?" "Will it interfere with something else I have to do?" and "Will I honestly feel good if I do this person a favor?" Don't be afraid of being too selfish. Many requests come when you do have the time and energy to do them graciously. Learning to say "No" when it's really inconvenient will help you feel even better about the times you do give of yourself. Better to be a cheerful giver sometimes than an overworked victim all the time!

Maybe your problem is the opposite: You tend to take advantage of others. Sometimes this is harder to spot, especially because it can be an unpleasant realization to face. The easiest way is to keep track of how often you do something for someone else and how often others do things for you.

If the percentage of time is not close to equal, you might consider whether you are being a vampire to your friends. Do you expect them to listen to you, but are "too busy" when they need to talk? If they provide help for you, are you available to do them a favor? At the very least, do you acknowledge their importance to you? (You can do this verbally, with simple gifts, or even an invitation out.) Sometimes we are so afraid of being taken advantage of that we slip into the habit of always thinking of ourselves first. Taking a good hard look at your actual give and take can be a very enlightening experience!

Whether you tend to be a victim or a vampire, there are danger signs you can look out for: (1) frequently being angry because someone hasn't done what you expected of them; (2) being so suspicious that you feel you can't trust anyone; and (3) feeling resentful of other people. Maybe you are being a victim and creating the situations that leave you feeling angry and resentful. Or maybe your suspicions and fears are leading you to be a vampire. Take a close look and see if your give and take are equally balanced!

Trust: How Much Is Enough?

Many people make the mistake of thinking that trust is an all-or-nothing proposition. They either trust someone or they don't. This means that if they are let down even once by a friend, they may decide that they no longer trust that person. Since none of us can always be there for our friends, this sets up the likelihood that we will end up trusting very few people.

A more realistic attitude might be to ask ourselves exactly what we can expect from a particular friend. Perhaps one friend is usually available when we need someone to talk to. Perhaps another friend has provided car rides when our automobile was broken down. Still another friend may have volunteered to provide child care in case of emergency.

No one person may be able to provide all these things, and none of these friends may be available every single time we need them. But if we are realistic about our expectations, we may realize that we can trust each of these friends to provide some support for us and to provide it most of the time we need it. We could use this information to feel very good about our friends. And if we feel we give these friends whatever help and support we are capable of, then we can feel very good about ourselves.

The problem of thinking that trust is all or nothing can lead to serious problems in marriage. Many people grow up with the mythology that their spouse will fill one hundred percent of their needs. Since this isn't realistic, they become angry and disillusioned. No trust is one of the most common complaints people have about an unhappy marriage. But often it is based on an unreasonable expectation that no human being could fulfill. By blaming the other party, people avoid examining their own demands. Until each person can state their requests reasonably and clearly, no negotiation is possible. The stalemate can be broken if each partner stops blaming and starts working together in a realistic manner.

One other mistake people make about trust is to think of it as based on externals. Trust is always a voluntary choice. We trust people because of how we feel, not because of what they have done. Before you argue with that statement, think of the number of times you have felt that you trusted someone you just met. Think of the number of people who still trust their friends in spite of occasional fights or misunderstandings. Think of how some people trust everyone, no matter what, and of other people who trust no one, no matter what!

Since we cannot predict the future with accuracy, and since we know no one is perfect, trusting someone becomes an act of hope on our part. It is a conscious choice to expect the best from another person. Before you say you can't trust anyone because of past experience, stop to ask yourself why you are choosing to give up hope. Each time you choose to trust, you are taking an active step to create a world of hope and faith.

Learning to feel comfortable being assertive about your own needs can make it easier to trust people. Being secure in the knowledge that you won't let yourself get stepped on can help you relax with other people. If you are not obsessed with the fear of being hurt, you can relate to others in a way that doesn't trigger their fears. Trusting yourself first makes it possible to choose to trust other people more often.

It is perfectly all right to say you trust a certain person "just this much and no more." It need not imply criticism of them nor a lack of friendship on your part. If anything, it can keep you better friends. It is far kinder to be realistic in your expectations, than to set the other person up for failure.

Can You Stand Having Enemies?

The fear of disapproval is one of the biggest obstacles in most people's search for a meaningful and well-balanced life. We get so caught up in living up to what we think others expect of us that we lose sight of our own needs and desires. If we criticize ourselves constantly, we are even more sensitive to the criticism of others.

Will Rogers may have never met a person he didn't like, but that isn't to say that everyone he met liked him! In fact, it is easier to feel good about people we meet when we aren't obsessed with wondering if they like us. You can learn to develop an appreciative tolerance (agape, if you prefer) towards people because you feel this contributes to the kind of world you want to live in. You don't have to do it because you want everyone to like you. Liking and being liked are two different things.

One reason for developing tolerance is so you can deal with people who hold views that are different or even hostile, to yours. Appreciating diversity can help you accord respect to other human beings even when you are arguing with them. You don't have to like people to respect them. This is why I prefer the word *tolerance* instead of *like* or *love.* You may not love your neighbors, but you can still treat them as you would have them treat you.

Fear of not being liked has nothing to do with respect and tolerance. Fear of disapproval can make you act in a way contrary to your values. It can make you hide your own feelings and refuse to speak up for your own needs. It can rob you of initiative and keep you from taking control over your own actions. In short, fear of making enemies can lead you to be dishonest with others and uncharitable to yourself.

The first question to ask yourself is why you are so frightened of having someone dislike you. If you are truly happy with yourself, then why should someone else's opinion negate all your good qualities? If you think someone who dislikes you could do you harm, then you need to determine whether this is a realistic fear. You also need to look at whether you are doing yourself more damage by being frightened. Why does it matter so much that one person like you?

The next question you need to ask yourself is whether the person in question is a potential enemy or just someone with a single complaint against you. Just because someone doesn't like a part of you does not make them a deadly opponent. Being so insecure that you cannot listen to criticism can make you rigid and defensive. Even your enemies can provide you with useful feedback as to how you come across to other people.

When people criticize you, look them straight in the eye and listen! Don't respond automatically by arguing, making jokes, or becoming angry or weepy. Hear what they have to say. Ask questions if you need to clarify their complaint. Don't assume they have ulterior motives or are out to destroy you. Don't make any immediate promises, but do let them know that you heard their criticism and will think about it.

Don't continue the discussion at this point. Be firm about taking some time to yourself. When you are alone, write down both your emotional and intellectual responses. Then review both lists carefully. Was the complaint justified? If not, why? If it was, what will you do differently in the future? If the way in which the criticism was given aroused strong emotions, can you suggest a less provoking way of giving feedback in the future?

When you have done this, and when you feel you can handle a discussion calmly, then respond directly to the person who was critical. Share your thoughts. Briefly acknowledge your feelings, but don't get hung up on elaborating on how you felt. Stick mostly with the ideas expressed. You don't have to agree with the criticism, but this procedure will minimize the negative impact of the discussion for both parties. It may even decrease some of the angry or hostile feelings.

People are not perfect. They will not always be tactful or kind. But then neither are you or I. Accept the fact that we all need to keep trying for a better world. Don't be discouraged, either by your own failures or the failures of others, from living up to the best that you are capable of. The only real failure is to stop trying.

If you want to make the world a little less lonely, remember that we are all connected by our relation to God and the world. Don't just complain; do something! Think of it as a challenge: How much good feeling can you encourage by your behavior? How much of an impact can you have? How much more pleasant can you make your little corner of the world?

Meaningful relationships can be encouraged by your efforts. Seek out other good people who are trying to become more sapient. Acknowledge that everyone is different and learn to appreciate the way God is manifested in our infinite diversity. Seek out people whose life experiences are different from yours and broaden your outlook.

Remember that the golden rule works to your benefit. Each time you extend fairness and respect to another human being, you improve the quality of your own environment. Develop a loving tolerance that lets you treat people well even when there is mutual disagreement. The disagreements may never go away, but they don't have to be accompanied by hate and hostility. Remember that virtues and faults are often two sides of the same characteristic and be gentle in your criticism of both yourself and others.

Don't let your hidden fears and prejudices affect your actions. When you act out of bigotry, the impact is felt throughout your company and your country. You're too smart to destroy an entire economy because you didn't take the time to think about what you were doing. One giant step toward putting meaning into your life is granting every human being the respect they deserve.

You don't have to be a victim or a vampire in your relationships with other people. Trust isn't an all or nothing situation. You can choose when and how much to trust. You can learn to give and take with grace. Life can be delightful if you can stop wasting energy on useless guilt and irrational fear of disapproval.

Don't let your fears poison your world. Don't ever forget the impact each of us can have. One of the characteristics of human beings is that we can dream something and then make that dream a reality. Concentrate on your hopes and that's the kind of world you'll help create. Concentrate on your fears, and they may become the reality. It's your choice!

Doing these things doesn't have to be a chore. It can be a joy. In Chapter Six, we'll look at play and try to understand how to put delight back in our lives. Sincere, spontaneous love comes only when we love ourselves first. When we are happy and secure, it is much easier to feel good about other people. If we rob our lives of joy and meaning, we tend to resent the happiness of others or see them only in terms of what they can do for us.

To put religion back into our lives, in its fullest sense, we need to be able to play as much as we work. All our activities can become part of the Universal

Dance, the active process of the Divine interplay within the Universe. We need to learn to be kinder to ourselves: physically, emotionally, and intellectually. Building balance into our lives builds meaning into them. And a sense of meaning is the basis of religion.

6

"Everything I Like Is Either ..."

Everyone in the country has heard the complaint "Everything I like is either illegal, immoral, or fattening!" It's the excuse most commonly used by people who aren't enjoying themselves. Yet it's an excuse that just doesn't make sense. Your favorite foods won't fatten you unless you eat too much of them. Illegal actions are usually prohibited precisely because they are dangerous or unhealthy. And things that are immoral or unethical involve harm to other human beings. (Some people specifically mean sex when they use the word *immoral*. In Chapter Seven, we'll look at the question of ethics as they apply to sex.)

Unless you really do only enjoy things that are hurtful to yourself and others (in which case, you might consider seeking professional help!), you probably want to reconsider this excuse. Why are you making excuses to avoid enjoying life?

Then again, maybe you're only using it as a meaningless excuse for your refusal to be happy. Maybe you just won't give yourself permission to play. Why do so many adults find it difficult to have a good time? Play is a way of learning, growing, and delighting in life itself. Without a sense of playfulness, we lose the perspective necessary for a rich and fully integrated life.

Why Can't Grownups Play?

As children we knew how to play. Everyday items could be a toy. A cardboard box became a castle. A sofa became an airplane. A stick could help us to climb mountains in our backyard or to beat a drum for a parade. Our own creative ability was the key factor. By using our imagination, the most mundane objects could help us be in another time, another place, even traveling through the infinite expanse of outer space.

Too many adults resent a child's ability to play. They try to squelch this gift. They refer to "just playing," as though it were of little value. Maybe these adults are jealous of the richness of possibilities that play presents to children. Children can try out new careers, travel to far away places, or be anybody they want to. The world seems to be filled with potential roles to play.

Too many adults feel trapped, as if they had no choices left in their life. Watching a child play, the trapped adult sees the child exploring infinite choices in her or his imagination. The adult who feels a lack of hope and freedom to make choices may transfer this negative feeling to the child. The adult who squelches children's play to "prepare them for the real world" is raising more trapped adults.

Why do we feel it is more realistic to look for the unpleasant in life than for the pleasant? Logic would tell us that the two extremes exist in equal amounts. But somehow there is a tendency for us to equate growing up with facing only unpleasant "realities." We often refer to someone as childish and immature if they display their emotions readily or use their imagination creatively. When we admonish someone to "Grow up!" we are usually suggesting that they stop being spontaneous and cheerful, and become grave and serious. You might think we equated being an adult with being pessimistic and emotionally guarded.

Is it really healthier and more mature to be pessimistic? Is the loss of hope really the price we have to pay for growing up? Does being "realistic" have to mean expecting only the bad and never the good? I have heard the proverb "Expect the worst ... and you'll never be disappointed !" From what I have seen of the human experience, you'll also never be happy!

The Effects of All Work and No Play

If you expect the worst, you are likely to create it for yourself. If you believe that growing up means working hard and shouldering burdens, you are unlikely to allow yourself time to play. Let's examine the results of an attitude of all work and no play.

If you see everything as a chore, if you expect drudgery from life, then you miss all the joy in everyday activities. If a cardboard box is just a container to mail a package in, you miss its connection with the rest of the world. If you are more worried about whether it is wrapped tightly and if the postage is correct, you forget it is also a magic carpet to other places.

Obviously, I don't mean that you should forget to wrap the package or stamp it. But if you then focus only on what can go wrong with its delivery, you ignore the fact that it is your connection with another place. Once you have carefully wrapped it and insured its safety, what would be the harm of imagining the pleasure of the people who receive it?

Perhaps you are sending the package as part of your job and have gotten so jaded that you regard it as a routine matter. What if you imagined it was a "pearl of great price" as you wrapped and sent it? Which "fact" is actually true? If you pretended it was of great importance and much depended upon its safe arrival, you would probably wrap it more carefully than if you hated the routine quality of the chore.

Do you really know the value of the package? Have you bothered to find out what it means to the people who are receiving it? Imagination can make a routine task more fun, and at the same time, help you to do the task better. If you were to pretend that the package mattered little, would you do a better job of wrapping it? Not likely!

The imagination that children use in playing a game can make everyday chores more enjoyable. Can you play that kind of game with yourself? If it troubles you to imagine that kind of importance in your routine tasks, you may be in the wrong job. Remember Shakespeare's line about the battle that was lost for want of a horseshoe nail. If you can't imagine the connections between the small things you do and their impact on events, you run the risk of feeling that you engage in meaningless tasks.

By devaluing what you do, you may have missed the importance of your daily chores. Your own pessimism may be the culprit. You assume what you do is of little value, and you fail to look for the connections. Is that really more realistic than accepting the fact that you may not see all the connections that are possible?

The danger here is in going to the opposite extreme, being overwhelmed by the potential significance of every tiny movement. Playfulness is the necessary antidote. If you are overly concerned with the importance of every move you make, you are likely to move very little. Your fear of making a fool of yourself or of causing harm can lead you to cease moving or growing at all. Only by developing a sense of playful enjoyment can you learn to move gracefully.

Think of our metaphor of life as a dance. It is true that every movement contributes to the overall beauty of the dance. But without the enjoyment of the dancer, the movements would be rigid and lifeless. The ability to be silly and playful counteracts the fear of falling or being clumsy and allows the dancer to try for leaps and twirls of greater and greater height and daring.

This is one of the paradoxes of trying to achieve a sapient life: you must simultaneously learn to see the cosmic significance in your life at the same time you recognize the wonderfully silly impossibility of ever living up to that significance entirely. You have to keep trying and be able to laugh at yourself when you fall. At one and the same time, you have to enjoy when you are living gracefully and appreciate the humor of the human condition when you are clumsy. Only the creative potential of your human imagination can help you cope with this paradox. But what a challenge if we try!

Learn to develop your imagination. Exercise it; don't let it wither away as you grow up. There's lots of ways to improve your creative ability. New experiences and new people can broaden your perspective. Read books that stretch your imagination. Play with your children, enter into their world of "let's pretend"; they can teach you a great deal about creativity. Experiment with ways to express yourself. Try writing, even if it's a journal that no one else sees. Crafts and hobbies can provide new ways of using your imagination. Learn the basics, then invent your own designs. Even sports and games can be a springboard to get you playing again.

Your imagination can make daily activities more fun, and special events even more special. Don't lock your creativity away with your childhood toys! Being able to play can improve your social relationships, your sex life, your job performance, and your overall happiness. In play, you can discover that sudden, spontaneous sense of connection that we ask of a religious life. When you are relaxed and happy and feeling that all's well with the world, you may find you understand life better than you could by using all the logical words in the dictionary!

The Martyrdom of the Mundane

Did you feel uncomfortable with the suggestion that you learn to play in order to really attain an integrated (i.e., religious) life? Harmony and balance come more often through joy than through suffering. But many people seem to prefer to believe that anything that isn't work is somehow bad. But feeling bad or unhappy doesn't improve the quality of your life or anyone else's.

The dictionary defines martyr as "one who chooses to suffer rather than give up his or her beliefs." The key word here is *chooses.* We're not talking about those rare occasions when someone is actually given a choice between their basic beliefs and death. We are talking about mundane martyrs, those people who choose to believe that the world is boring and hurtful. By expecting the worst, they refuse to look for the best. By expecting to suffer, they refuse to allow themselves to enjoy.

You may know people like this. They are always complaining about the sorry state of their lives. What is worse, they tend to blame others for their misery. They hate their jobs, but they can't get a better one because of the state of the economy. They're working themselves to death to put the kids through school. They know they need to lose weight or stop smoking or drink less, but how can they when they can't cope with all their problems. If you ask them why they don't do something drastic to improve their life, they will very likely shrug their shoulders and say, "That's life."

You can usually spot mundane martyrs by their air of resignation. They have lost faith that life has meaning. They have given up hope that life can be any different. Is it any wonder that they so often find it difficult to be charitable to themselves and to others? Yet they are choosing to suffer because of the beliefs that they hold: the belief that life is a painful struggle, the belief that adults should "take life seriously," the belief that play is silly and unproductive.

We have discussed repeatedly the way in which people create the reality they believe in. The self-fulfilling prophecy is one of the key abilities of human beings. We are the only inhabitants of this planet who can think about things that don't exist and then create them. Unlike animals, we don't just respond to the world; we create it. We give it form by the way we perceive it. In our relatively short time on earth, we have had a greater impact on the environment than any other species.

Maybe part of the reason for the negative impact we have had on the environment is because we have stopped "playing" with it. We have given up the old mythologies of wood sprites and animals who bring messages from the divine. We have replaced it, in many cases, with an "objective" view that studies nature while distancing it from us. But treating nature as an object does not insure that we treat the environment with neutrality and fairness. When we cease projecting a friendly image on nature, we also cease from recognizing our interdependence with it.

There will be many people reading this who will protest that logic alone can tell us that we have to treat the environment with more respect. But serious logic has not had that impact on our behavior. Only when rational knowledge is combined with a positive emotional response does the desired impact permeate all levels of a human being. Maybe the old folk tales and mythologies can't be brought back; maybe they shouldn't. But some more playful and imaginative perspective must be introduced if we are to stop viewing our lives and the life of our planet with such disregard.

The Modern Version of the Temperance Movement

I have strong reasons for thinking a sense of play must be incorporated into our attitudes if we are to attain a more balanced and religious existence. Over and over I have seen people who act according to logic, but who have lost the joy of their actions. Instead of martyrs, they have become missionaries. And both attitudes are equally stifling and unbalanced. Replacing the values you have learned from society with the value derived from logic doesn't solve the problem of despair. Without a sense of play, neither one can provide a healthy feeling of connectedness.

Let's use food preparation as an example. It is an action which must be performed if we are to physically survive. Like other biological imperatives, however, it can be expressed in countless ways. We can make cooking and eating a joyful event or a depressing chore. We can enrich it with meaning or devest it of all significance. You express your entire world view in your mealtime habits.

You can avoid meat on Fridays or keep the kosher dietary laws because you were told to. Or you can do these things because they remind you of your connection to other people in your spiritual community. You can choose to say a blessing over your food because you are really glad to be eating it or because "God will punish me if I don't." A playful attitude can often make the difference. Someone who sees these dietary suggestions as rules is likely to feel limited by them. Someone who sees them as reminders of significance may feel excited and challenged by the prospect of abiding by them.

Being able to play can make all the difference. If you delight in exploring new and enjoyable ways of sticking to these suggestions, you make them an inspiration rather than a prison. Enjoyment is meant to be a part of eating, as it is meant to be a part of all our life experiences. Vegetarians who cook tasteless food are as lacking in harmony as gluttons who gorge themselves on excessive quantities. Members of religious groups who keep food restrictions joylessly, out of a sense of duty, are hardly gaining grace for themselves. To deny the pleasures of life is to deny life itself.

Many people today take up a cause without integrating it into all levels of their life. They quit smoking, give up caffeine, or become vegetarians, all for the healthiest and most logical of reasons. But if they have no joy in what they have gained, one has to wonder about their hidden motives. Rather than using their energy to attempt to argue other people into applauding the virtue of their actions, they might provide a better example by clearly enjoying their new habits. An ex-smoker who can now cheerfully play his or her favorite sport longer or a vegetarian who prepares delicious and nutritious meals is doing more to encourage good habits than any number of missionaries and their verbal arguments.

All too often we complain about the way in which someone else lives, without being consistent in applying these criticisms to ourselves. If you criticize the use of alcohol but use pot or LSD regularly, you are being hypocritical. Wouldn't it be more honest to admit that we are all looking for easy ways to feel good? The next step would be to admit that getting high on life itself would probably be more healthy than using any kind of chemical to create a synthetic pleasure. And instead of condemning those you know who use any kind of drug, first ask yourself if you set an example of enjoyment and grace that provides a desirable substitute for chemical highs. The answer to the problem of chemical abuse (whether caffeine, nicotine, alcohol, or psychedelic) is teaching people how to feel so good about their lives that they don't need to escape from them.

Many people drink or smoke in order to provide an excuse to relax and be silly. Instead of feeling free to play in constructive ways, they resort to a socially excusable way of escaping their everyday life. Aside from the physical damage they do to themselves, they hurt their ability to become sapient because they fail to take an active role in putting joy in their life. They rely on the influence of the drug and never learn how to play without it. They are like birds who never learn how to fly.

Learning to Create Balance in Your Life

One of the first things we can do for ourselves is to stop pretending that we ever grow up. Some people act as though adulthood is some magic plateau that we reach suddenly, at which point we are complete. They may see another stage beyond this, a place called "old age," where we gradually lose our adultness and deteriorate until this second childhood is mercifully ended by death. If we diagrammed their view of life, it would look like this:

The "over the hill" life plan

Adulthood

Childhood   Old Age

It seems likely that people who look at life this way are condemning themselves to a rough climb, a short stay at the top, and an inevitable decline. Because this is what they expect, they will fit every new experience into this framework. They may see reaching adulthood as leaving childhood behind. As Peter Pan said,

> *"growing up means it would be*
> *beneath my dignity to climb a tree."*

The joy and exploration of childhood are seen as something to discard in the climb to being grown up.

Worse yet, once at that peak stage, every indication of the approach of the declining years is dreaded. Forgetting a name or an appointment may be ingored in adolescence; you were too busy to remember. But forget a name or appointment when you are thirty or forty, and you may find yourself fearing the onset of senility. We may forgive some imperfection in ourselves when we are young, but make a mistake in adulthood, and you may feel like relegating yourself to being over the hill.

What if we were to develop a more realistic life plan? Given the self-fulfilling nature of our concepts, wouldn't a different framework create a different feeling in our life? Of course it would! So let's look at another way of thinking about life's journey.

Human beings are born incomplete. Unlike other animals (our purely earthly relatives), we are born helpless and lacking in basic survival skills. Because we have been granted a sapient aspect as well as an earthly one, we are born incomplete so that we can develop that wisdom. If we were born nearly finished, there would be less room for motivation or growth. Interaction with the environment and the caring people around us allow us to grow far beyond the purely earthly inhabitants of this planet.

Perhaps the true meaning of the proverb "God helps those who help themselves" is that we can grow only if we participate in the growing. Learning is an active process, and there seems to be no limit to the learning of which humans are capable. In other words, we can work with God to complete ourselves. We are not created with fully realized potential; we have to participate in the process of developing our potential.

The real significance of our lives may lie in that participation. We will never be complete or finished (at least not in this world). But if you believe you were created by a Divine Being, then striving to develop and grow means that you are working in partnership with the Ultimate Source. There may be no fixed limit because the real meaning of your life consists in seeing how far you can go and grow in this lifetime. Every year in your life contains new experiences, new chances to grow. Each stage in your life is a chance to learn something new, to develop new potential. The process is never over, but the act of growing is more important than whether you ever reach a final goal.

If we were to diagram this view of life, it might look like this:

The "journey of exploration" life plan

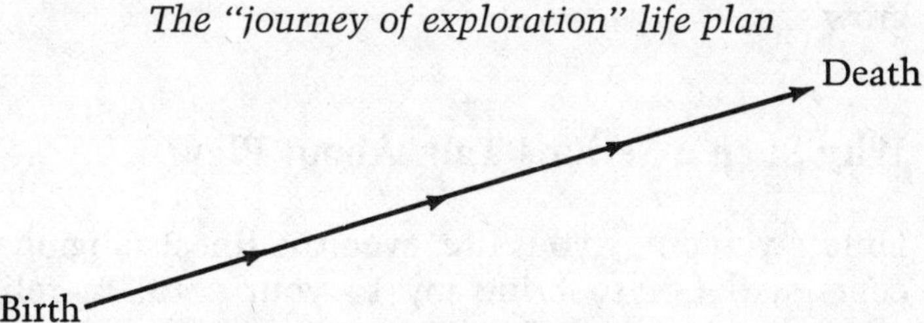

If you believe in a life after death, you may wish to add to the diagram. Just be sure that you don't make the afterlife your major goal! Focusing on expected rewards after life keeps you from focusing on life while you are living it. If you believe that God created everything with a purpose, than life itself must have more significance than just keeping us from death.

If you believe that we are reincarnated so that we may continue learning, you have but to fold this page into a circle and the diagram becomes a three-dimensional spiral to illustrate the continuing process. In either case, you have something to look forward to, unlike the "Over-The-Hill" Life Plan, in which death is, at best, a way of stopping the downward trend.

This "Journey of Exploration" framework might also be called the "Something New Every Day" model. By focusing on the importance of all of life's experiences, it reminds us that every day presents new experiences to learn from. Even if you expect to be doing the same things today that you did yesterday, you can take the initiative in doing them better this time. And if every day in your life seems too much the same, this model provides an incentive to go forth and seek new experiences. After all, each new person or event provides more opportunity for growth and learning. Work on your share of the partnership with God by encouraging yourself to grow.

Why Such a Serious Talk About Play?

Unless you enjoy your life, even the finest religious concepts will fail to bring joy to your soul. In religious mythology around the world, the soul has been symbolized as something lighter than air. The very word *spirit* is related to the Latin word for *breath*. It inspires our life and lifts us above a purely physical perception of our world. Play and laughter feed the spirit. They can add lightness to our lives and keep us from becoming weighed down by routine activities. They can prevent our being overwhelmed by the sacred or bored by the profane.

Enjoying our own life can make it easier for us to share in the joys of others. Play can make the most difficult task easier. The hardest part for most people is giving themselves permission to play. But we have to value joy enough to allow it into our lives. If we don't make creative use of our imagination, we may end up having to numb it with chemicals or give in to despair. Learning how to play constructively is a valuable investment of your energy. The reward is being able to transcend earthly limitations.

Divine meaning is elusive. It cannot be forced. In order to perceive the true significance of life, it is often necessary to live it first and understand it only later. We need to plan ahead to encourage those things that have meaning to us. But then we have to live life, to work and play with zest and enjoyment, and to accept the unexpected. Each time we have new experiences to adapt to, we can again take a rest from the dance, in order to plan which directions to take next.

It is this pattern of participating, then analyzing, that can give rhythm to the dance of life. You cannot plan ahead for every possibility. There is always new knowledge to be learned and unexpected challenges to meet. By stopping for a breathing spell between parts of the dance, you can learn from past events and prepare for future ones.

The dance is never finished until you cease to move. There is no limit to how much you can learn. Living a joyful life can be the fullest expression of your religious views, whatever they are.

7
Sex, Sin, and Sanity

Sex is probably the most difficult topic to deal with in a discussion of religion. Instead of telling us how to become more comfortable with our earthly bodies, most organized religions have treated sex as dangerous and sinful. Yet if religion is supposed to help us uncover the meaning of our existence, how can it ignore or condemn such a basic human drive? But some people will react with fury even to the suggestion that an honest and practical religion must accept the joy of sex. We are faced with the problem we discussed in Chapter One: that of putting certain areas of our life into separate boxes and refusing to apply the same standards uniformly.

Your attitudes towards sex have an impact far beyond such sexual behavior as intercourse. They affect your treatment of yourself, especially the way you feel about your physical body; and they affect your behavior toward other people, especially those of the opposite gender. You may be protesting at this point that you are quite comfortable with sexuality and think of all people as equal, regardless of their gender. If so, let's try a little experiment.

Go back and reread one of the first chapters in this book, substituting the word *Goddess* for *God.* What are your gut-level reactions when you do this? Be honest with yourself; this can be a very enlightening exercise! How far would you have read in this book if I had used the word *Goddess* whenever I referred to a Divine Being? Yet if you believe that all people were created in the Divine image, then surely the word *Goddess* should have been just as acceptable.

After all, the Divinity that we are talking about is really so complex that any image is a poor description. If I speak of "God the Father," I am doing the Deity a disservice by using such a limited picture. We are told that the Divine Being is all things and more, eternally young and eternally old, understanding and experiencing all. Therefore any title is bound to be just a small part of the infinite reality. Yet I have seen enough raised eyebrows (and sometimes raised hackles!) when God is referred to as "She," to feel the depth of our prejudice against an integrated Divinity!

On my wall is a Hindu poster that illustrates the all-encompassing nature of God. A male and a female figure are joined in sexual union while their countless arms and legs participate in the many activities of the universe. The picture is so complex that many Westerners do not notice the details at first. When they do, their first reaction is often one of disgust or leering embarassment. Yet this Hindu depiction of Divine participation in life's activities is less limiting than a Western icon of a bearded man, whether on a cross or on a throne. How can we accept the infinite complexity of the Deity when we refuse to accept our own complexity?

The process by which we eat food and transform it into our own body might be seen as a marvel of creativity. How clever a way to provide for the growth and regeneration of a complex organism! You can marvel at the process whether you attribute the origin to Divine Planning or Natural Law. Sex is just as marvelous a process. How clever a way to draw us closer together, to reconcile our differences, and build mutually pleasing relationships! We can delight in our earthly bodies, which can provide so much emotional and interpersonal joy. We can even see sex as a metaphor for the integration of our physical and nonphysical aspects, since touching inspires feelings far beyond mere physical sensations.

I am not arguing for any particular image of God, but rather for an acknowledgment of the Divinity in all aspects of our humanity. If you can only visualize God in one limited aspect, you run the risk of denying all other aspects. If you can't imagine God in a female aspect, even for the sake of an experiment, then you run the risk of denying the Divine spark in women. (This is true whether you are male or female. Many women find it extremely difficult to acknowledge the female aspects of the Deity.) Obviously, the reverse problem would occur if you could not imagine the male aspects of God. However, this is much less common in our society.

If you have always visualized God in one particular form, you may want to try this exercise in creative religion. For the next month, every time you pray, imagine God in a different form: female, male, black, white, Oriental, old, young, all the diversity you can think of. You may develop a new humility or a new pride, depending on how much like you your usual image of God was. You may find yourself regarding the people around you with a new respect. And you may come to a new understanding of what God is: not a distant being but a living presence.

Men and Women Come from Different Cultures

Let's imagine for a few moments that you are an alien from another world. Earth is a totally unknown planet, and you have been sent to gather information about its life forms. Watch the interactions of men and women. Notice the differences in dress, behavior, and actions. You will see women dressed in high-heeled shoes that make walking difficult and skirts that inhibit free movement. You will notice that, in accordance with this nonfunctional style of dressing, women are accorded less functional roles in the business world. They tend to be paid less for the same work than men. They are underrepresented in upper management and politics. They are more often found in the company of children than men are, and they tend to do menial maintenance chores more often than men. Even the Divine Spirit that both genders worship is almost always portrayed as male.

Notice how each gender communicates. Women speak more often about feelings; men about facts. People show their disapproval of a woman when she displays anger; they show their disapproval of a man who displays tears. If he takes off his shirt, it indicates that he is working hard. If she loosens any article of clothing, it may be taken to indicate a sexual request. He can curse under stress; she risks social disapproval if she uses the same words. If he goes out for a drink after work, he's "one of the boys"; if she does, she's a "loose woman."

Notice the miscommunications that occur when they attempt to communicate with each other. She wants him to talk to her about how he feels; he considers a friend "someone you don't have to explain things to." She says, "We never do things together!"; he responds, "What do you mean? We watch TV every night together!"

You might argue that you know people who behave differently than this. But when our objective alien tallies up the data, the above examples are the statistical norm. Well, now we recognize the problem. Men and women are living in two different worlds. We raise them differently, teach them different values, and encourge different behaviors. Then we neglect to provide a universal translator. No wonder they have problems understanding each other!

This inconsistency causes trouble precisely because men and women need each other. Sending us to separate planets would not only result in the disapperance of our species, it would also result in many very unhappy and frustrated people! Sex is the epitome of ths dilemma. We desire sex, we need other people to enjoy it fully, and yet our problems in communication about sex cause some of our greatest heartaches.

Why do we have such difficulty dealing with a desire that should act to bring us together? How do we twist a binding activity into one that drives us apart? The answer lies in our own ambivalence towards sex. Too often we isolate sex from our other aspects and avoid examining our attitudes with an almost paranoid intensity.

Some Modern Paranoias Concerning Sex

Nowhere is our ambivalence toward ourselves displayed as clearly as in our attitudes toward our bodies.

Obviously there are the extremes of people who tend only their bodies and neglect their soul, just as there are people so concerned with spirituality that they ignore their bodies. Both attitudes reflect a lack of balance.

But many people seem to swing between opposing views of their own physical humanness. People who believe that we are created in a godlike image may also believe that showing that image is sinful. People who believe that "the body is the temple of the spirit" may also feel that the activities of the body are evil. People who believe in the sanctity of life may also shorten their own lives with the indiscriminate use of chemical poisons.

Being unable to integrate all the different parts of ourselves can lead us to great confusion. Most religions have spent as much effort on regulating the physical aspects of life as they have on developing the spiritual aspects. It is as though they see body and soul as enemies.

Some religious groups also set up mind and soul as enemies, as though thinking could weaken spirituality. This book is committed to the idea that the use of the mind can enhance religion by helping people to integrate their beliefs with their everyday actions. In this chapter, we will focus particularly on the direct expressions of the body, such as health and sexuality.

If we are truly the "earthly wise ones," then our earthiness must be part of our heritage and gifts. To set our physical side at odds with our spiritual side denies us the chance to be comfortable with all our characteristics. The two aspects of our humanity do not need to be at odds. Historically, many of the religious prohibitions on sex were derived more from social and political needs than from a spiritual necessity.

Denying an aspect of one's own being is not the way

to achieve balance and harmony. Nowadays we have enough scientific knowledge to recognize that going without bathing or wearing the same clothes for months on end are not a display of sanctity, but rather a public health hazard! During the Middle Ages, the measure of sainthood might have been the extent to which a holy person ignored his or her body.

Witness a certain saint in the Middle Ages. Upon his death, his clothes were so encrusted to his body with months of dirt that they had to be cut off. If he believed that his body was made in the image of God, I wonder how he explained to his Maker why he treated that godly image so badly! His behavior doesn't seem to illustrate harmony and comfort with being human.

Standards may be changing in the area of cleanliness as related to godliness, but our attitudes toward the sexual activities of our body are often still archaic. I once read a science fiction story in which an alien culture treated eating as a shameful act, to be done in privacy and secrecy and never talked about. Is our attitude toward sexuality any less culture bound?

We take a natural and necessary physical behavior and enshrine it in artificial restrictions and taboos. It has mystery and magic inherently, for the process of emotional bonding and species preservation is as complex and marvelous as the process by which we consume food and transform it into our own living cells. Sex is as much of an everyday miracle as eating. But we treat one as dangerous and the other as trivial.

We will talk about the sanctity of eating (and sleeping) later on in this chapter. Right now, let's see if we can bring some logical and realistic light into the area of sexuality. In other words, we can try to integrate the body with both our intellectual mind and our spiritual beliefs.

If you listen to common usage of the language, you will realize that we use the word *morals* most frequently to refer to sexual behavior and reserve the word *ethics* for other usages. We judge sexual activities by an arbitrary set of proscriptions and reserve rational ethical analysis for all other kinds of behavior.

Some people who have read this far with enthusiasm may suddenly want to back away. There lurks an irrational fear in many hearts that being logical about sex will somehow destroy moral fiber or cause some other vague disaster. It is as though they see sex as an overwhelming force that needs to be restrained or it will break loose and dominate our lives. It is a shame that this fear prevents us from looking at sex rationally, since I doubt our behaviors would change for the worse. My hope is that they would change for the better.

For example, most people simply state that sex outside of marriage is sinful and immoral. This doesn't necessarily stop them from engaging in sexual activities with people other than their spouses. It just means they sneak around like children stealing from the cookie jar. Since being sinful is a value judgment on their whole being, they waver between trying to justify the act as not sinful (in which case, they aren't bad) or feeling guilty and miserable about themselves as people.

If we removed the moral judgment, we would then be able to view the action logically. If you have made a contract with your spouse that you will both be monogamous, then breaking the contract is a breach of ethics. It has practical consequences that go along with breaking any contract. Your credibility is damaged. You may be in the position of having a conflict of interests that interfere with your living up to the rest of your contract.

You are not damned, nor is it an unforgivable action.

But it does have a negative impact on a significant partnership in your life. If you have been thinking realistically instead of simply going along with preconceived assumptions, you probably choose monogamy for a number of reasons.

You promised one person your primary attention in exchange for his or her primary attention. You know how difficult it is to give attention to one intimate relationship if you are distracted by another. Since sex builds bonding between humans, you wish to reserve your primary bonding for your spouse. Monogamy insures that the children of the relationship are the children of both spouses. You are making a statement about with whom you wish to spend most of your time. You can probably list many more reasons for your choice.

If the decision for monogamy was made for a number of practical reasons, then breaking the contract may not be in your own best interests. Not because it is a sinful act, but because it will hurt the relationship between you and a person you depend on.

Some people make a different contract. They do not promise sexual monogamy, but do promise that the majority of their time and energy will be spent with their partner. Often they find out that this can be difficult. Since sex tends to create an emotional bond between people, they are often faced with the choice of starting a bond which can grow no further or trying to keep sexual partners casual.

While it is possible to enjoy sex just on a casual and nonemotional level, it goes against the human tendency to want to be loved with intensity. Many mature and caring people find that monogamy occurs, not because it is forced upon them, but because it brings more joy and less pain than nonmonogamy. It is hard enough to develop a deep and growing relationship with one person. Adding other relationships to cope with only steals energy from the primary relationship and makes all bondings more difficult.

The problem with making sex a sin in some situations is multiple. First, many people continue to associate sex with sin in all situations. This makes it difficult to enjoy or to think about rationally, even with loved ones. Second, it is no more logical to consider the act of sex a sin than it is to consider the act of eating or sleeping a sin. All are natural needs of the human body.

Third, simply stating that sex is a sin prevents people from learning to accept responsibility for it. They are so busy hiding from their "sin" that they fail to develop the ability to consider their actions and the consequences in a practical manner. Fourth, it makes it impossible to accept being human in a positive manner.

And fifth, it prevents us from acknowledging and rejoicing over a very special miracle. We cannot appreciate and make the best use of something if we feel ambivalent about it. And that is a waste of a god-given ability!

Toward a Morality Based on Ethics

When people refuse to deal honestly with their sexuality, they usually have trouble applying normal ethical standards to their sexual relationships. Normally, we judge our behavior as bad if it hurts ourselves or others. But when it comes to sex, too many people throw these guidelines out the window.

The problem with concepts of morality is that they

are usually arbitrary and impractical, if not downright destructive. If you define sexual activity as immoral, except between husband and wife, you are focusing on the least relevant factor. (Before you stop reading at this point, let me elaborate!) This kind of rule implies that sex is generally bad, with a grudging exemption made for married couples. It defines an activity such as masturbation as immoral, despite its usefulness in maintaining both physical and emotional health. The logical extension of this rule would suggest that really "moral" people could do without even this exception (as has been suggested by religious writers in the past). The focus of this rule doesn't encourage pleasure. It does encourage seeing marriage as a prison and ignores any ethical responsibilities between husband and wife.

By contrast, imagine a morality based on ethical guidelines, such as defining sexual activity as good when it provides positive results for the people involved and does not cause harm. This focuses on the pleasing aspects of sex, the ways in which it can draw couples closer together. It makes sex within marriage a desirable goal, since sexual activity repeated with one loving partner increases intimacy and can enhance physical enjoyment. It discourages the trivialization of sex, since that minimizes the potential benefits of sexual activity. Treating people purely as sex objects usually results in negative emotions for one or both parties and can have a destructive effect on interpersonal relationships.

Defining the limits of sexual activity in these ethical terms doesn't prohibit sex outside of marriage. It does emphasize that a responsible, considerate attitude is important to good sex, under any conditions. If we stopped disapproving of sex in general and started disapproving of dishonest or demeaning sex, it might be a more pleasant and more consistent world. How many times have you been offended by somebody who overtly condemned sex outside marriage, but leered approvingly at an acquaintance who had an extramarital affair?

We tend to be particularly ambivalent toward women who admit their sexuality, even if we think we are liberated in our attitude toward women in nonsexual settings. For example, if a woman openly acknowledges enjoying sex, people are likely to stop treating her with ordinary courtesy. Without knowing the actual details of her life, they make assumptions about her selectiveness or the frequency of her sexual activities. Rape is far too often seen as a case of "she asked for it," than as an act of violence by the male. The fact that a woman or man is willing to indulge in sex does not mean she or he relinquishes the right to be selective about the choice of a partner.

The Body as Temple

When we regard our bodies with ambivalence, we are less likely to treat them with proper care. It is reassuring to find so many people today who are concerned with what they eat and whether they are getting enough exercise. Unfortunately, many of them seem to be doing it as an exercise in self-discipline, rather than an experiment in self-pleasing. Too often they seem to be focused on punishing or changing themselves, rather than the sheer enjoyment of having a physical body.

Your body is a home for your personality, a temple that reflects the divine spark within you and a living, moving expression of your individuality. Bathing it, caressing it, feeding it properly, are all ways of appreciating the physical aspect of your humanity. Improving your body through care and exercise can be done to repair past disrespect or to enable your body to cooperate more gracefully with what you ask of it.

Take the time to look at how your actions reflect your attitude toward your body. How do you feel about your physical self? Do you hate your body? Were you told it was bad when you were a child? Do you shower quickly, trying to avoid parts of the body that you were told not to touch? Or do you allow yourself to enjoy a lingering hot bath, relishing the feel of the soap caressing all portions of your self? Do you enjoy the strength and agility of your body when you exercise, or is working out a way to punish yourself for having a body? Do you allow yourself to enjoy the taste of good food, the comfort of eating just enough, and the health that comes from a balanced diet? Or do you stuff or starve yourself beyond comfort with a careless disregard for the quality and quantity of that with which you nourish your body?

All too many people today have been deluded into believing unrealistic stereotypes regarding the "perfect" body. We believe in an image that is entirely fictional. Few people beyond the age of twelve really have a flat stomach, male or female! Barbie dolls have a pathologically unhealthy body shape, and extra muscles do nothing to improve a man's social techniques, in bed or out.

The greatest harm in chasing the unreal is the damage we do to ourselves in the process. Instead of liking our own body as it is and developing our own individual potential, we compare it to the unreal and end up with a severe case of self-dislike. Then we get sidetracked on a program of starving and stretching that distracts our energy from the real areas where our potential needs developing. We torture ourselves with "self-improvement" plans, when we really have no realistic idea of what kind of improvement would bring us happiness and peace. We seem to be a nation of psychic masochists!

This confusion over "self-improvement" often triggers a multitude of insecurities and creates conflict where none need be. For example, in recent years, there has been quite an upswing in the number of books published on how to masturbate. Some people see this as a moral decline and the first step into a depraved, narcissistic society. Others argue that it is a sign of our entry into a future of physical pleasures that will banish emotional problems from our minds. People polarize because of their basic uncertainties about what their existence means.

The increase in books on self-pleasure doesn't have to be seen either as certain doom or certain paradise. In fact, they often have a far simpler motive. There has been a growing recognition that unless you love yourself, you cannot love another. If you are ashamed of your own body, you cannot truly rejoice in the body of someone you love, nor can you approve of that person rejoicing in you. Pleasing oneself can never take the place of joining with another human being in love. People who care about people often find masturbation dull; like eating in fast-food outlets, it's convenient but lacking in substance. But unless you can take pleasure in yourself, you are unlikely to be able to join with someone else in sharing without reservation.

Thus, the majority of these books are both a symptom of our despair and the expression of hope. They need to be written because too many people are uncomfortable with their body the way it really is. And they are an exercise in raising your consciousness of your body. They are not a cure-all, but they are not depraved either. They simply ask you to become acquainted with a part of you that you may have been ignoring, your physical self.

The above is an example of how a simple exploration of our human characteristics can become an exciting topic only because it provokes our existing uncertainties. In practical terms, the point is this: If you find yourself strongly repulsed by or strongly attracted to books on sex, consider your response. Maybe you're angry because they are asking you to deal with your unresolved repulsion toward your own body. Maybe you are interested because they promise a solution to your unhappiness with your own body. In either case, the resolution isn't in the book, it's in understanding yourself better. The desire to burn a book you don't like is really the desire to destroy your own uncertainties. True religion means coming to terms with your internal conflicts, rather than leaping to attack or defend a particular topic just because the topic upsets you.

If the body is a temple for the Divine spark in all of us, then treat it that way. Don't make it a dead memorial; live in it and enjoy its beauty. Don't poison or pollute it through ignorance or ignore-ance. Consider, once again, the concept of partnership with God. If you own your body in partnership, what is your share of the responsibility? Will you say, "I tried to ignore it; I was ashamed of enjoying it"? Will you say, "I was careless; I often damaged it"? Or will you resolve your conflicts enough to say, "It's beautiful; I enjoyed it immensely, and I tried to take good care of it"?

Dis-Ease and Dis-Stress

Let's talk about another partnership: that between your body and your mind. To be ill at ease or unable to handle stress can have severe effects on your body as well as your mind. Many people have trouble recognizing that body and mind truly work together. You can probably recognize the effect that physical actions can have on your feelings. Talking a walk on a sunny day or playing your favorite sport can make you feel good or tired or both. But have you noticed the many physical changes brought about by your feelings? Feeling embarassed makes blood rise to our cheeks. Feeling angry can make the muscles in our stomach tense or our fists clench. Fear can make our palms sweat. Nothing we do is purely physical or purely emotional. Mind and body are constantly interacting.

Stress is being blamed for countless health problems today. But *stress* simply refers to the effort of interacting with the environment. All stress is not bad; a certain amount of challenge and change stimulates you to keep growing. When doctors talk about stress-related illnesses, they are referring to the results of poorly managed stress. How we perceive and handle stress is the most significant factor in determining whether we will feel dis-stressed.

When you are faced with stress, your body automatically responds. Muscles tense. Blood vessels to the skin constrict. Digestion slows down. Heart rate speeds up. We breathe faster and our blood pressure goes up. Our biochemical balance changes, too. Adrenaline is pumped into the bloodstream. Blood sugar levels increase. Hormones alert the nervous system to prepare for action. Most, if not all, of these changes occur before you are even aware of them. Your mind perceives stress, and almost instantaneously your body responds.

It's quite an effective partnership! It happens so unconsciously that we tend to forget how closely mind and body are connected. When we ignore this connection, we can abuse the body accidentally by provoking this stress reaction unnecessarily. Every time we tell ourselves something negative and pessimistic, we are causing ourselves stress. Every time we ignore our emotions, we are raising our stress levels. Every time we feel frustrated, angry, or worried, we cause our body to respond with changes that can be damaging. The longer these negative emotions linger, the more harm can be done.

We are learning more and more about how we function as whole individuals, and how dis-stress and dis-ease are the opposite of growth and inner harmony. What is important now is how we use this knowledge. For centuries now, our focus has been on using science to conquer the external world. Once we began to develop the scientific method, we began to accumulate knowledge about what things are made of and how they work. But we turned so much to seeing the world as composed of things that we began to see ourselves as things too.

Like machines, we demanded to be fixed if we were broken. We asked science to dehumanize us. We demanded pills that would make everything better, without any effort on our part. We demanded that people called "scientists" and "doctors" collect knowledge and dispense it only as needed. We didn't try to understand the whole picture ourselves; we created a split between science and ourselves. But science (*i.e.*, knowledge) isn't enough. Wisdom is needed. And wisdom demands an internal focus.

We have denied responsibility for what happens to

us, and in doing that, we have done ourselves great harm. No pill can repair the damage that a lifetime of neglect can do to your health, no more than clean-up programs can keep pace with the amount of poison we unthinkingly dump into the environment. In short, no amount of knowledge can repair the damage we do if we refuse to accept responsibility for healing ourselves.

It doesn't require the accumulation of vast amounts of knowledge to create a better world; that knowledge is there already, collected in libraries and laboratories and in the minds of those people who explore special areas of interest. But it does require the wisdom to accept the responsibility of connecting all that knowledge in a coherent way. We often complain that it is too hard to keep up with scientific knowledge, and that experts don't agree anyway. But each "expert" is only a worker in one particular area, with one particular perspective. We have to take the responsibility to hear each perspective, and put them together in the healthiest way possible. Our lives depend upon it.

We have to take responsibility for healing ourselves by treating our bodies with love and respect and by handling our thoughts and emotions so as to encourage positive growth, not negative dis-stress. We have to learn to work in partnership with doctors, treating their knowledge with respect but not expecting them to step in to wave a magic wand and save us from the effects of our own neglect. We need to question them more, recognizing that their training has given them only one perspective. They are human too, and if they reach immediately for a pill or the knife, we must realize that they sometimes seek to resolve their own uncertainties by reaching for an easyanswer.

All too often we see accepting responsibility as a painful chore. But it is really a joyous expression of hope, for it is the only way to have an impact on the future. Instead of blaming our problems on outside sources, we need to develop an internal focus of responsibility. Instead of looking for easy answers to physical, emotional, and environmental health, we need to recognize that the real solution is to work with the rest of the world to resolve our difficulties.

Sex isn't a sin; treating people as things is. Illness isn't an act of God; it's usually a consequence of our own lifestyle. "Experts" aren't to blame for the sad state of the environment or the economy or world affairs; we are, for abdicating our share of the work needed to improve these situations. The knowledge of science isn't enough to create sane, healthy, happy lives for all of us. That knowledge needs to be coupled with the wisdom that comes from a truly religious sense of our interconnectedness with the rest of the universe. The meaning of our existence is the recognition that we are creating our world in partnership, a cooperative effort of people, nature, and God.

To deny the need for that cooperative effort is to provoke soul-sickness. To label the mere accumulation of knowledge or the building of technological objects as "progress" is to create a house of cards that will eventually topple of its own weight. True progress will occur when we use that knowledge and those objects to improve the whole world, not just our little portion of it. Because all life is interconnected, we do not actually have a little portion all our own. If we pollute the air and water, we poison ourselves. If we eliminate illness, but fail to develop health, we die anyway. If we fight constantly to keep the peace, we have not stabilized anything. And the worst part of all will be the knowledge that we did it to ourselves. What an irony it would be if our share in creation was the destruction of everything!

8

Whatever Happened to Miracles?

One of the saddest conflicts that has arisen in our society is over the loss of miracles. We seem divided into two opposing extremes: those who deny the numinous entirely and those who believe in miracles indiscriminately. Instead of being a topic of wonder and joy, a discussion of miracles often provokes fanatical opposition. Why does this occur? Is this not another area in which the sacred and the profane must again be balanced?

Many religious organizations have given up all ritual and beauty in order to make their ceremonies less mysterious. Yet beauty is found in complexity as well as simplicity, and that which is difficult to understand can sometimes provide more raw material for the imagination than the sterile timbers of pure logic.

Science is a way of thinking, an approach to understanding. But it is a mistake to think that what we can see, touch, or measure is the whole of the world. Science can bring knowledge, but not necessarily wisdom. There are people who seem to think that knowing how something works takes away its miraculousness. I may marvel at the intricate workings of a beautiful clock. Watching the craftsman at work building it or seeing a blueprint for its parts does not change it.

It remains a miracle to me that the clockmaker can plan ahead, craft each piece with care, fit them together, and still develop beauty to match the function. I marvel at the minds of humans that we could invent such a thing, our hands that we could build it, our hearts that we could see its beauty. All the knowledge I receive about the clock only enhances my appreciation of the miracle of its creation. How much more so for the miracles I see each day beyond the abilities of any human?

Coincidences, Miracles, and Divine Providence

There seems to be a running battle between people who value imagination and people who don't. Like children at play, some people can look at clouds drifting across the sky and see cavorting animals or exotic landscapes in their shapes. But other people refuse to see the world as a giant Rorschach inkblot; they want clouds to be clouds and nothing else.

There seems to be a number of problems inherent in scorning imagination. First, it seems to be a uniquely human ability, and scorning a characteristic that makes us human seems suspiciously like self-scorn. Second, human culture is built on imagination. Everything in art and science is the product of someone's imagination, someone's dream made concrete. Third, denying the imagination leaves one with tunnel vision, unable to see anything outside of the direct line of sight. A non-imaginer wanders through life handicapped. Fourth, because all skills need to be exercised to develop, non-imaginers run the risk of having their imagination wither. Eventually they forget how to use it at all, even when they need it to solve a problem or to cope with despair. And fifth, life just isn't as much fun without it!

If we think of imagination as the skill which lets us take mental leaps and see the connections in the universe, we can see why it is such a wonderful human characteristic. It enables us to write a novel or paint a picture and allows us to formulate a theory and design the experimentation to test it, and makes it possible to dream of something that doesn't exist and then invent it. When we use imagination in such productive ways, it becomes easier for many people to accept its value.

But not all of us create imagination-inspired products that can be enjoyed on a large scale. What functions, then, can imagination serve for us? It can be used to enhance everyday living, as we cook, dress, or arrange our living space to provide the most delight and the most benefit. It can be used to enhance social relationships, as when we try to understand how another person feels, and then devise new ways of interacting with that person to improve our communication. And it can be used to help us see the ever-present connection between ourselves and the universe itself.

One of the problems with failing to use our imagination to see the interconnectedness of all things is exemplified in our attitudes toward psychic events. We talk about the paranormal and the supernatural. We treat these kinds of events as though they existed outside the "normal" and the "natural" order of things. We may treat them that way so as to more readily pretend they don't exist at all. Or we may treat them that way so as to not have to think about them in a more realistic manner.

People who read the horoscope listing in the newspaper every day are not using their imagination; they are abdicating it. They are lacking in wisdom as much as the skeptic who refuses to even consider the existence of psychic connections. Both groups are simply showing prejudice; they have made certain assumptions and refuse to question those assumptions. Each side goes out of its way to look for arguments to support its position, ignoring all information that might threaten their prejudgment.

Consider for a moment the amount of experimentation done each year in the field of parapsychology. Each year scores of experiments are done to test the hypothesis that people are sometimes able to obtain information in ways other than through the five physical senses. For the last hundred years or so, experiments of ever-increasing rigor have been done, and positive and negative results accumulated to add to a growing body of information.

Consider only those whose experimental controls are at least as good as those in other scientific laboratories. Numerous well-designed experimental procedures have demonstrated statistical results far beyond the predictions of probability theory. But these results are largely ignored, remaining unintegrated into either mainstream academic thought or the thoughts of average people.

The two exceptions to this refusal to assimilate the data are again examples of polarization. Those hostile to any positive results expend a great deal of energy looking for particular examples that may legitimately be criticized for less than perfect experimental controls. Those friendly to positive results tend to read little of the legitimate experimentation, but accept any claim to paranormal abilities as proof of their preexisting beliefs.

While critics look for flaws and ignore the main body of data, believers welcome any spoon-bending or table-tilting fraud with open arms. Each side finds it easier to accept all claims that agree with their position, rather than to make the effort to deal with the actual data, which is less one-sided. The truth is that the laboratory results are often subtle and show up only through statistical analysis.

The ability to be telepathic, precognitive, or clairvoyant is limited by numerous factors, including the subject's attitude, the frame of mind they are in at the time of the experiment, their physical or psychological comfort, and many other factors. People who claim to be able to manipulate information or objects on a large scale are most often using physical methods to achieve their objectives, either consciously or unconsciously.

Psychic effects seem to occur in a way consistent with what we know of our world and our functioning within it. How we think and feel affects psychic phenomena the way it affects everything else we do. Attempts to produce effects that violate too many other forces, such as the pull of gravity or our physical inability to pass through solid walls, have so far been unsuccessful. Psychic processes seem to be just one of the many tendencies and dynamics at work in the universe. Most often we do not notice their discrete effects because they are just a small part of the many influences affecting us constantly.

But this is exactly what is disappointing to most people, scientists included. I suspect that we ignore the results of parapsychological studies not because they are too shocking, but because they aren't shocking enough.

We insist that we'll believe, if only we can see an event that violates natural law. We don't want to believe that the miraculous is a part of natural law.

The dictionary defines a miracle as "a wonderful happening that is contrary to or independent of the known laws of nature." Does that mean that when you learn more about the previously unknown laws, the event becomes less wonderful? Is a miracle less wonderous if it is beautifully articulated as part of the known universe? Is it no longer a miracle because it is consistent with the harmony of the world, rather than striking a discordant note?

It's almost as though we want miracles to be in a category outside our existence. We may want to dismiss them as aberrations in the natural order. Or we may want to think of them as interventions that rescue us without any effort on our part. In either case, it often suits our hidden agenda to insist that miracles be large-scale, obvious, and totally inconsistent with the rest of the natural world. We define them in a way that makes it impossible for them to occur!

It is possible to define miracles slightly differently. Miracles may be seen as wonderful happenings that reflect the interconnectedness of the universe. If you are most comfortable using the word God as the spirit of that interconnectedness, then miracles become an example of Divine Providence, God's constant relationship to each individual. Events in which you see meaning become reminders of the universal connection among all things.

Those who dismiss meaningful events as "mere coincidences" are not only depriving themselves of a chance to be reminded of the cosmic connection, they are indulging in meaningless rhetoric. We use the word *coincidence* to refer to events that occur at approximately the same time and appear to have significance, but for which we can see no direct physical connection. Isn't this very similar to our dictionary definition of miracles? We don't yet know how the events occur, but we marvel at their apparent meaning.

If someone were to ask me how to distinguish between a pathological belief in the supernatural and a healthy recognition of life's interconnectedness, I would suggest that that person apply the same analysis that should be applied to other beliefs and assumptions. Does the belief encourage growth and a broadening of outlook, or does it result in a narrow and stifling world view? Does it help in dealing with other people, or does it result in an intolerance toward other perspectives? Does it add richness and meaning to the individual's life, or does it isolate and diminish it? The real test of any belief lies in the examination of its practical effects; "By their fruits shall ye know them [Mt. 12:33]."

The Difference Between Knowledge and Wisdom

You have to have a certain amount of sophistication to perceive a miracle. First of all, you have to have a particularly human kind of wisdom to realize that the Divine Meaning is manifest throughout the universe. Second, you have to have the imagination to see the connections that exist. An animal who bumps into a clock left in the forest doesn't marvel at it, because the animal doesn't have the imagination to see its complexity and implications.

Those who actively look for meaning are more

likely to find it than those who don't. It takes practice in making connections. It takes practice to allow yourself to see the reflections of the cosmic connection without forcing your projections onto the universe. It takes a subtle combination of actively exercising the imagination, using your reason to keep yourself in balance, and being able to be receptive to Divine reflections without distortion.

Humans are capable of experiencing a sense of wonder and joy. This is related to our ability to play, because we are talking about feeling delight over things that have no immediate physical survival value. In other words, an animal may feel some pleasure at receiving food when it is hungry. But only our species experiences delight over "toys" for the mind, concepts like truth and beauty. Being able to play means being able to appreciate the world for more than just its ability to provide food and shelter. As a species, we need this play so much that we even create our own art and culture to express this imaginative appreciation.

God has been likened to The Ultimate Artist, who creates the artwork with great subtlety out of preexisting materials. It takes great imagination to see the potential in that which exists and to bring forth that potential beauty. Life is not suddenly created with a violent catastrophe or inconsistent action, but formed with a gentle shaping of the old to produce the new.

It seems like the ultimate arrogance for us to suggest that God is supposed to do things differently. If we insist that creation must be sudden, not evolving, we are essentially arguing with Divine methods. We may be displaying the same hubris when we insist that God forgive our sins immediately, instead of recognizing that the burden is on us to start building wisdom and consistency into our lives. Instead of demanding that the meaning of our lives be revealed to us in miracles that violate the Divine harmony, we could start working with God now to build meaning and significance into our world. Only by seeing our role in the cosmic partnership can we develop our full potential.

Mystics of every faith have often been accused of magnifying insignificant things out of proportion. They tend to see wonder and significance in everyday events. They marvel at miracles at which we close our eyes. We fail to recognize that calling everyday things "insignificant" is minimizing events out of proportion. If we recognize that we aren't all-knowing or all-wise, then shouldn't we refrain from pretending we can make this kind of judgment? Isn't it more practical to assume that the smallest events have significance and to do things in a way that encourages positive consequences for even the smallest actions?

The Logic Behind the Nonrational

Humans are the only animals who dream of what doesn't exist and then create it! It has been said that we even create God in our own image, rather than the other way around. Maybe a more accurate way of viewing this phenomenon is that we describe the Divinity with words and metaphors that reflect our limitations. We do not usually comprehend the total reality of God. It may be that we cannot. But these limited metaphors can bring us to grief and further fragmentation.

If, for example, we think of God as "Ruler of the Universe," we are suggesting an image of God that reflects a particular human style of relationship. But Nature reflects God quite differently. Nature is better described as an organism, rather than a kingdom or a machine, constantly growing, each part gently interacting with every other part. Were we not so influenced by our culture, we might describe God as "Gardener of the Universe," or "Artist of the Universe." Different images of the Divine Principle might encourage us to change our value system to one more appropriate to a dynamic partnership, rather than a feudal kingdom.

To remember dreams or to forget them may be the ultimate human question. We can pretend we exist alone, without purpose and meaning. We can pretend there is no other reality than what we can see directly before us. We can pretend we have no responsibility beyond immediate sustenance. We can deny our partnership with God. And by doing so, we can create a self-fulfilling prophecy in which we cease to exist as human beings.

Maybe the myth of the Garden of Eden is a prophecy, rather than a memory. Instead of describing the past, maybe the myth describes a possible future in which our indiscriminate consumption of the fruits of the Tree of Knowledge destroy our world. If we use our technology unwisely, with a total disregard for good or evil, we may blow ourselves out of Paradise abruptly.

Both logic and imagination are needed to design a life that simultaneously feels good and results in constructive consequences. A feeling of playfulness and enjoyment about participating in the challenge of living is a good indication of a balanced life. It often seems easier to lose yourself in seeking pleasure or drown yourself in gloom. Balancing both joy and a positive impact takes more effort. But the results are infinitely valuable.

We know that the two hemispheres of the human brain process information differently. The left side of your brain arranges things in a linear, sequential way. It helps organize facts, perform logical analyses, and translate thoughts into verbal speech. The right side of your brain processes data in a more imaginative and wholistic way. It perceives things simultaneously, makes intuitive leaps, and understands concepts like spatial relationships and music in a nonverbal way.

You might think of your left brain as oriented toward science and language, and your right brain as oriented toward religion and artistic expression. With your left brain you can stand apart from events and observe them analytically. With your right brain, you can experience events fully and participate in them emotionally. Without both hemispheres of your brain, you wouldn't be fully human. Yet in Western culture we have tended to overdevelop the skills of the left brain and underutilize the capabilities of the right brain.

Because of this undervaluing of the whole potential of the brain, we have allowed techniques that develop particular brain functions to become associated with specific spheres of study. Studying science can help you learn techniques of logical analysis. Studying religion can help you learn techniques of meditation. We do not make a concerted effort to teach all students techniques to develop the functions of both sides of the brain. Yet scores of great scientists have shared their experiences in which intuition helped them make their greatest creative leap. And members of the clergy are aware of the need for logic to help them translate their experiences into practical guidelines.

The average American is left handicapped by an educational system that overdevelops one set of functions and often discourages the development of a complementary set of functions. Yet we cannot be whole unless we develop the skills of both sides of the brain. Part of the reason for the epidemic of soul-sickness, of meaninglessness, is due to the atrophy of those human capabilities that help us perceive the universe in a wholistic and intuitive way.

This deficiency has come to be recognized in recent years. In a piecemeal way, we are trying to remedy the situation. Courses in meditation and creativity are becoming popular even among business populations, traditionally the most conservative and the most over valuing of logic. But there is little systematic attempt to integrate these techniques into a basic life plan or to increase the overall value right-brain functioning has in our society. Courses designed to develop right-brain skills still remain the stepchild of most curriculums.

Ironically, organized religion has often fallen into the very trap that our culture in general needs to escape from. In an attempt to become relevant and progressive, many churches and temples have discarded the very specializations they have been safeguarding all these years. Meditation techniques that seem too mystical, rituals that seem too much like magic, folk traditions that seem too illogical, are all discarded as embarassing remnants of the past.

But meditation techniques can be a valuable way of developing right-brain functioning. Rituals can help shift our normal consciousness into a state more conducive to perceiving the cosmic interconnectedness. And folk traditions help link us to both past and future and remind us that our normal perspective is limited by our own mortality. Instead of discarding all these techniques, what is really needed is to encourage their use in a way that helps us develop all our potential, compensating for past cultural deficiencies and allowing us to become fully functioning Homo sapiens.

The irony is that the people who display the most painful signs of soul-sickness are the least likely to follow up on the practical implications of this. Tell someone who feels hopeless to try meditating, painting, sculpting, or dancing, and they may protest, "I don't need a hobby; I need purpose!" Tell someone who is working themselves to death joylessly that they need to alter their state of consciousness, and they may complain "That's just for flower children and bums!" Yet the paradox is that learning to play without purpose is an excellent first step toward recovering the lost parts of yourself. It is the nature of life itself that we sometimes need to recognize opposites before we can achieve balance and harmony.

Stasis and Ec-stasis: A Sapient Approach

Nature is always in motion; it only looks still because of our limited sense of time. Like a dance, it hesitates, then leaps. Like the tides, it ebbs and flows. Stillness is just the space between movements, and movement just the space between pauses. Our mortal human perspective does not always allow us to see this flowing harmony. Our limited perceptions can work to our disadvantage. In one person's lifetime, that person may not realize the changes that are occurring or the impact that each person has. Our imagination can help us leap beyond that limitation of time and mortality to recognize the significance of our everyday actions.

Perhaps we can think in terms of static and dynamic patterns of relating to the world. Let's use the Greek terms *stasis* and *dynamis* to avoid any preconceived values we might place on the more common terms in use today. The word *stasis* has the various connotations of *peace, place, equilibrium, rest,* and *physical mass.* The word *dynamis* has the various connotations of *force, movement, energy, strength,* and *vigor.* Inertia is stasis; momentum is dynamis. Accumulation of knowledge is stasis; insight bursting forth is dynamis. It should be apparent that the universe is not one or the other of these concepts, but rather the interaction of the two opposites: taking in and giving out, observing and participating, being loved and loving, the yin and yang of life itself.

Life itself is composed of these two principles. Separating them out, even for the purpose of talking about life, is artificial. They don't exist separately, but only in relationship to each other. Our human characteristics include the ability to perceive opposites as existing simultaneously, for only by accepting this paradox can we function at full capacity. When we develop all aspects of our human potential, we can make the leap outside our usual place and experience both sides of the paradox of life at the same time.

Indeed, in this state of consciousness, this ec-stasis (that is, transported out of the static), we may transcend time as well as space and simply perceive our vast connections with the cosmic. This leap, this trance, this ecstasy is at the heart of the religious experience. But it is an experience that cannot be fully translated into words, because it is more an experience of the right hemisphere of the brain than of the left. The role of the logical left brain may be to help us use this right-brain experience to transform our daily life into some reflection of our transcendent experience.

This thought disputes the popular view that religion is a mysterious world where reason cannot penetrate. Logical analysis can certainly be applied to religious thought, but this kind of knowledge is not the same as the experience of the numinous. We may experience a religious experience; logic can help us translate that experience into everyday life, as we have been attempting to do throughout this book.

Reason is not in opposition to religion; logic adds to the positive impact of a person's total world view. But it is only a part. Imagination helps us see the connections; logic helps us integrate that insight into our lives. Logic without religion is sterile and meaningless. Religion without logic can deteriorate into dogma and fanaticism.

Making enemies of reason and religion is a symptom of our own fragmentation. It means that we have been too lazy to make the effort required to integrate the two viewpoints. Since Homo sapiens appear to be the one species capable of thinking in both scientific and religious terms, it may be that the ultimate expression of our sapience is a life that integrates these two extremes of thought. To succeed in developing all the potential of our human heritage, we cannot just ignore half our capabilities.

The resolution to this dilemma may be found in the ability to shift perspectives. But this ability, although innately human, can wither from disuse. If we persist in developing only certain aspects of our human abilities, we will not become fully human. If we continue to see ourselves as fragmented and trapped in many boxes, we will not pull ourselves together into whole and healthy individuals. If we cannot reach ourselves to recognize the cosmic connections that surround us, we will continue to feel isolated and despairing. If we cannot be sapient, we will perish from the sickness of our souls.

To dance with the universe is to be filled with joy. To work with God to create the world is to live up to our full potential. Miracles exist to inspire us when we are tired. It takes less energy to be a wallflower in the dance of life, it is true, but it brings no rewards. The joy is in the participation.

9

The Living Congregation

When people are discussing ways to integrate religion fully into their lives, the question inevitably arises: "Isn't it easier to do this if you move into a religious community and give up the world entirely?" There are two reasons why I don't think it is easier. The first is that the real challenge in being sapient is to live your religion while *in* the real world. Too many peole seek to escape the experience of life, rather than to meet it head on. Gautama Buddha returned to the world after achieving enlightenment; Jesus Christ lived among everyday people for the most significant portion of his life. It may be more difficult to hold on to your faith in the mundane world, but your impact is greater.

The second reason is that the attempt to live one's religion, in the final analysis, is a very personal quest. My experiences lead me to believe that there are more potential dangers of becoming too identified with one particular group, ideology, or "guru" than there are benefits. Putting your unquestioning faith in any human or group of humans is a poor substitute for exploring your own cosmic connections.

The key word here is *unquestioning*. Giving up your ability to question or analyze your beliefs means that you give up your right to actually integrate your religion into your life. Following someone else's words blindly is no more "living" than heating a TV dinner is "cooking." If what someone else has said (or is saying) is valid, it will remain so, even if you examine it carefully. And you will be actually participating in your religion, not avoiding it.

Remember that there are two sets of functions of which the human brain is capable. Besides being able to logically analyze and adapt your religious beliefs, you need also to be able to feel them. No one else can experience God for you. Without a real sense of the cosmic interconnectedness, beliefs can become sterile and joyless. If you are used to only mundane consciousness, it may take some effort on your part to learn how to alter your state of consciousness enough so that you can see the world from a different perspective.

Churches, Covens, and Communes

The conclusion that religion is basically an individual affair is based on the years I've spent studying specific religious groups who have tried to live apart from the rest of society. I've met saints and charlatans, public and private psychics, ministers and magicians. I've met people who gave off a quiet aura of being genuinely holy. I've met the leaders and followers of communes and lamaseries, bible-reading groups, and magic circles. Despite the apparent diversity in the content of their religious beliefs, some patterns reoccurred in everyone's daily life.

Every group I've ever studied has had a mix of good people and not so good people. No matter what the religious focus, some people within the group seemed to function better than others, in social relationships, in ability to be productive and self-supporting, in their feelings of self-worth. Not a shocking finding, certainly, but one that argues against the idea that living in a religious community automatically makes it easier to be healthy and holy.

Furthermore, there were always certain disadvantages present. In varying degrees, individual communities had to deal with the problem of integrating themselves into the larger community. The tendency to see the world as "we" versus "they" was usually intensified. In most cases, the less contact an individual within a community had with the outside world, the less practical and realistic their life style appeared. Those who were most successful in social relationships and ability to be self-supporting often expressed frustration at those members who were unable to function without the group's support.

Convenience is often cited as reason to live with groups of like-minded people. Farmers, homesteaders, and people who live off the land need other people to pool their efforts for seasonal tasks and shared problems. People with dietary restrictions (vegetarians, those who keep Kosher laws, *etc.*) can be more comfortable in communities that don't discourage their eating patterns. The problem is, we could make the same case for environmentalists, recyclers, and almost any other category we like. If convenience were the goal of living, it would follow that we should all live only with people who live like we do.

But the convenience of living with people who agree with you is overbalanced by the danger of becoming self-righteous and ethnocentric. Under such circumstances, community beliefs often degenerate into orthodoxy, and individual deviations may come to be regarded as heresy. Besides such pressure to maintain the dogma of the status quo, religious orthodoxy may become more valuable than the ability to be practical in providing for the physical necessities of life.

When adherence to religious convictions leads to inability to support oneself, refusal to respect the rights or needs of others, and inability to form close and interdependent relationships, the religious convictions cannot be said to be integrated into a healthy life style. Although in every case studied, there were varying degrees of difficulty in integrating religious principles with everyday economic concerns, those who were at least minimally successful in the outside world usually displayed healthier behavior patterns overall.

To put it in simple terms, there appears to be no direct correlation between strength of religious belief and health or happiness. However, people who attempt to balance the two (*i.e.*, religious and earthly concerns) often appear to function better in both spheres. If it seems more difficult to achieve such a reconciliation of opposites, then the irony is that those who choose the more difficult task often come closer to developing their full potential.

The conclusion I have reached is that while it is easier to withdraw from the world in pursuit of religious principles, it achieves nothing. True partnership with the Divine consists of trying to manifest your principles while still in the world, which is itself a manifestation of the same Divinity. If withdrawal from the real world is the way to express religious feelings, then death would be the ultimate religious expression! Life is given to us as a way of developing our potential; if we fail to recognize the cosmic interdependence while alive, we waste the gift of life and express our contempt of God.

Ritual, Reality, and Relevance

Some people continue to live in a diversified world, yet still share their special feelings with other people. This sharing is one of the finest motivations for organized religious groups. The sharing of rituals and traditions can provide inspiration and support without requiring complete withdrawal from the larger society.

Some people feel that religious rituals are silly or meaningless. That's too bad. They can be the most play-filled part of religion. For one thing, they often link us to the past and the future and give us a sense of the cosmic perspective on time. They can remind us that our questions and needs are the same ones shared by other humans throughout the span of our existence.

Rituals help us celebrate. They serve to remind us to feel joyful and keep us from getting trapped in the mundane world. They can lift us out of our ruts and reintroduce us to symbols that stir nonverbal feelings within us. They have an important place in our lives because they stimulate the functions of the right hemisphere of our brain.

As with our intellectual beliefs, rituals need periodic evaluation if they are to remain relevant. Yet this is not to say that they should be discarded just because their origins are far in the past. Traditions that have been passed down for centuries can be enormously powerful. But they need to be questioned so that new answers and interpretations can become associated with them. This keeps them more vital and relevant than if they were regarded as fixed and unquestionable. We all have a need for mystery and beauty, if only to remind us that mystery and beauty can exist in the world. Rituals can be a dramatic example of that and can stimulate thoughts and feelings that may not be easy to express in words, but give meaning to our lives nonetheless. Like all art forms, the experience is worth a thousand words.

Do We Know Our Own Priorities?

We're a strange society. The elven o'clock news programs hand us a grab bag of information each day: world news, local crimes, weather, sports results, current movie reviews—all lumped together with equal volume and emphasis. Sometimes I've wondered if an alien could sort out our priorities by watching these shows. The sportscasters often seem to show more intensity than the announcers telling us about events which affect our very existence.

Sometimes we need to stop and think about our priorities. Instead of just taking in information all the time, we need to evaluate. Instead of just reacting and adapting to every new situation as it comes along, we need to plan in advance where we are going. If you don't want to manage your life "by exception," you need to have a consistent internal focus to keep you on target.

Research studies have established the fact that workers show greater productivity when they are shown how their individual role affects performance within the entire company. In other words, people work better when they have a sense of the meaning of their work. We all need to ask ourselves "Where am I going?" "What is my place in the team?" "What is the team's place in the world?"

None of us can survive in a world without other humans. It isn't just a question of avoiding loneliness. As humans, during our long childhood and adolescence, we learn by identification with others, first parents and family members, then other significant people we come in contact with. There is no such thing as a human being outside the social environment. We derive our human nature and our individual personality from social relationships. We achieve our own identity because of our emotional fusion with others we have known.

We grow, as well, from our interaction with the rest of our environment, but we often learn our style of growing from the people around us. Our choice of jobs, home, marriage partners, and so on, are all influenced by what we have experienced through other people. Whether we are trying to rebel against those people or emulate them, we still act in relation to their actions.

But this often leaves unsatisfied needs inside of us. To truly grow to our fullest potential, we need to grow in relation to a larger experience. We need to see beyond the people we know or the neighborhood we live in. We need to transcend the immediate if we are to transform ourselves into everything we are capable of becoming.

This need to grow is one of the chief characteristics of the human species. Transforming ourselves is a greater achievement than transforming Nature. We need to come to an acceptance and loving tolerance of our own human diversity before we attempt to impose limitations on our physical environment. Because we still tend to dislike people who are different from us, we cannot deal holistically with Nature, which sometimes appears very different from us. Until we learn to live the golden rule, we will continue to see both other humans and Nature itself as our enemy.

If we really came to recognize our close interdependence, we would project a friendlier image unto Nature. We are subjective creatures; our existence is constantly structured by the way we think about things. We have what linguists call "displacement," the ability to think about that which is not there. We create a model in our minds and then impose that structure upon the world, even to the extent of building things that did not exist. If only we focused on creating our dreams, rather than our nightmares.

Maybe we overvalue our importance. We are not the most important beings in the universe. We are not the goal of Nature. Maybe we assume importance only as we earn it, as we become active and constructive partners in creating the universe. We must judge our meaning and value, both collectively and as individuals, not by what we are, but by how we act. Learning to live collaboratively in the "real" world may be the ultimate challenge we all have to face.

Historically, the development and progress of a species usually leads to greater specialization. Then change occurs, and if a species becomes too specialized to adapt, it may become extinct. What lessons will we learn from this? We are in danger of being specialized for competition, thus producing our own extinction. We run the risk of being unable to adapt to a world that needs cooperation on a global scale.

Part of the role of God in our lives may be to insure randomness and play. If the world were perfectly ordered and perfectly stable, what would be the role of Homo sapiens? All our unique gifts and potential would be meaningless. There would be nothing for us to do except to conform to the universal order. The purpose of play may reflect the role of the Divine play—to provide a chance to actually participate in the building of the universe. Events may be random, in that they cannot be expected or predicted. But I do not believe they are ever random in the sense of being without purpose. Without the unexpected, we would have no chance to grow to our full potential.

Earlier on in this book, we asked whether we expect more of a relationship than the other person is willing to give. We discussed the need for ethics in friendship and courtship. Are we as thoughtless with God as we sometimes are with other people? Do we think Nature owes us a living? Life is collaboration and adaptation. If we persist in treating the world as if it were made for our convenience, we will be throwing away our chance to cooperate with creation.

It has been said that life defeats our efforts to understand it. Perhaps that is because its meaning is in the living of it, not the explaining. Life can only be partly expressed in words. We have been given all the capabilities of both halves of our human brain so that we can experience all of life's richness. As long as we keep exploring our capabilities to live, there is always more to appreciate. Religion, by stressing our cosmic connections, helps remind us of that infinite gift.

No one is ever complete, finished, or perfect. Instead of causing us to feel hopeless, we should rejoice in our unlimited potential. We can always grow fuller and more complete. There is always something new to experience that can add to our picture of the world. When people ask me (sometimes with a smile and sometimes with a disapproving shake of their heads) "What do you want to be when you grow up?" I have one basic answer: "I'll never be finished, so I'll keep being new things until the day I die (and maybe even afterwards!)" Each life is a marvelous work of art that is never finished, but grows more beautiful and complex day by day.

Living Your Religion in the Real World

Throughout this book, the emphasis has been on living your religion in the real world. This has led us into exploring many diverse topics. But each of these areas needs to be brought into focus if we are to achieve an integrated life. Let's review our path so far.

First, we asked ourselves some questions on what it means to be human and to be a religious human. We explored the symptoms of soul-sickness and agreed that we need to develop a particularly human kind of wisdom—sapience—to heal ourselves. Then we examined the ways in which we could be wiser.

We threw ourselves right into the workplace, despite the fact that it is often the most difficult place to remember our cosmic connections. We tried to explore our needs and desires and ways to improve our image of ourselves as we work. Most of the questions and exercises in Chapters Two and Three could be used to explore other areas of our lives as well.

Then we reexamined the golden rule and looked at its implications. We recognized the need for truth and honesty in all our dealings with people, including with ourselves. In Chapter Five, we looked at some of the ways we hurt ourselves by ignoring the rights of others.

We tried to understand why it is so often difficult for us to feel joyful, and we evaluated our need for play. By comparing life to a dance, we realized the need for both logical planning and spontaneous expression. For those who are rusty at the dance, we suggested ways to develop those right-brain skills they had ignored.

Because we are "the *earthly* wise ones," we needed to take a look at how we feel about the physical aspect of ourselves and how those feelings affect the way we treat others (sex) and the way we treat ourselves (health). If our body is a temple for our spirit, we realized the need to treat it as such.

From the physical, we moved to the completely spiritual, those dreams, mysteries, and unphysical happenings which human beings are capable of experiencing. We tried to find a balance that would allow us to appreciate the unexplainable without handicapping our efforts to function effectively in the physical world.

Finally, in this chapter, we have explored the ways in which we can share our religious convictions with others without losing our tolerance for diversity or removing ourselves from reality. In some ways, this has been a presumptuous book. It has attempted to encompass the range of human experience into an integrated whole in just a few words. But the guidelines we established have proven valuable to many people. And if they prove valuable to even some readers, this book has accomplished something.

And that, perhaps, is a metaphor for our lives. We try to share our experiences so that others may learn from us. We provoke discussion so that we may learn from others. And together we try to rediscover those universal interconnections that help show us our place in this world. We may recover some spark of the Divine as we express our perception of life's meaning. Like this book, our lives are never complete or perfect, but the real satisfaction arises from knowing that we have tried to work together to express the cosmic connections.

Bibliography

Daniels, Madeline M., Ph.D. *Realistic Leadership* New Jersey: Prentice-Hall, Inc., 1983. Written from a business perspective, this book contains practical techniques for "spring-cleaning the mind" and achieving better relations with friends and co-workers.

Edwards, Betty. *Drawing on the Right Side of the Brain.* Boston: Houghton Mifflin, 1979. An excellent set of techniques for actually learning a new perspective on the world. Meant for doing, not just reading!

Eiseley, Loren. The author, a distinguished anthropologist, writes about human development and nature with a childlike wonder at the marvels of life, and a scientist's understanding of their complexity. Some of his works include: *The Immense Journey.* New York: Random House, Inc., 1957; *The Firmament of Time.* New York: Atheneum, 1960; *The Mind as Nature.* New York: Harper & Row, 1962; *The Unexpected Universe.* New York: Harcourt, Brace, & World, Inc., 1969; *The Invisible Pyramid.* New York: Charles Scribners Sons, 1970.

Fowler, James W. and Robin W. Loving. *Trajectories in Faith.* Nashville: Abingdon, 1980. The life stories of five famous people are used to illustrate the development of faith. You may not agree with Fowler's theory of the stages of faith, but this is a book to make you think.

Gaylin, William. *Caring.* New York: Aldred A. Knopf, 1976. The author argues that humans are fundamentally caring creatures, and by using this impulse creatively, we can transform ourselves and our world.

Koestler, Arthur. *The Roots of Coincidence.* New York: Random House, 1972. Subtitled "An Excursion Into Parapsychology," this book brings together some thoughts on science and philosophy, and points to the need for a revison in our current concepts of both.

LeBoeuf, Michael. *Imagineering.* New York: McGraw-Hill, 1980. This book provides a summary of just about every technique known for enhancing creativity. The emphasis is on producing practical ideas that you can apply.

Ullman, Montague, M.D. and Nan Zimmerman. *Working with Dreams,* New York: Delacorte Press, 1979. Another book of practical techniques for finding out what your unconscious is trying to tell you.

Watts, Alan. These books, written by one of the great philosophers and religious "integrators" of modern times, are thought-provoking and can help break down some of the artificial boxes you may have created. Here's just a partial list (most available in paperback from Random House):
Nature, Man and Women. New York: Random House, 1970; *The Book on the Taboo Against Knowing Who You Are.* New York: Random House, 1972; *Psychotherapy, East and West.* New York: Random House, 1975; *The Way of Zen.* New York: Random House, 1974.

Wolf, Fred Alan. *Taking the Quantum Leap.* San Francisco: Harper & Row, 1981. This book, a layperson's guide to modern physics, may just convince you that fact is far stranger than any fiction! Very readable.